DRIVING CHANGE THROUGH DIVERSITY AND GLOBALIZATION

DRIVING CHANGE

THROUGH DIVERSITY

AND GLOBALIZATION

Transformative Leadership in the Academy

James A. Anderson

Foreword by Ronald A. Crutcher

STERLING, VIRGINIA

Sty/us

COPYRIGHT © 2008 BY
STYLUS PUBLISHING, LLC.

Published by Stylus Publishing, LLC
22883 Quicksilver Drive
Sterling, Virginia 20166–2102

Library of Congress Cataloging-in-Publication-Data
  Anderson, James A. (James Alan), 1948–
    Driving change through diversity and globalization :
  transformative leadership in the academy / James A.
  Anderson.—1st ed.
        p.   cm.
    Includes bibliographical references and index.
    ISBN 978–1–57922–098–3 (cloth : alk. paper)
    1. Multicultural education—United States.
  2. Education, Higher—Curricula—United States.
  3. Education and globalization—United States.   I. Title.
  LC1099.3.A53   2007
  370.117—dc22
                                              2007011282

EAN (cloth): 978–1–57922–098–3

Printed in the United States of America

All first editions printed on acid free paper
that meets the American National Standards Institute
Z39–48 Standard.

Bulk Purchases

Quantity discounts are available for use in workshops
and for staff development.
Call 1–800–232–0223

First Edition, 2008

10   9   8   7   6   5   4   3   2   1

To the transformational leaders who have shaped my values and vision on diversity:

Kermit L. Hall (in memoriam)
Larry Monteith
Hilda Richards
John Welty
Ronald A. Crutcher
William E. Kirwan
Ben Ruffin (in memoriam)
Reginald Wilson
Marlene Ross
Fred Carrier
Craig E. Nelson
David Schoem
Derrick Scott
Johnella E. Butler
Laura I. Rendon
George D. Kuh
Carol Geary Schneider
Jean MacGregor
Barbara Smith
Marilee J. Bresciani
Willard "Bill" Lewis

CONTENTS

"The problem of the twentieth century is the problem of the color-line—the relation of the darker to the lighter races of men in Asia and Africa, in America and the islands of the sea." Thus wrote W.E.B DuBois at the dawn of the twentieth century. Arguably, one can state that two of the most vexing challenges of the twenty-first century are related to DuBois's statement: They are the dual challenges of diversity and globalism. Diversity, of course, remains a vestige from the twentieth century—a challenge for which we in higher education have been unable to find effective solutions. Even those who have not read Thomas Friedman's 2005 book, *The World is Flat*, should recognize why globalism is such a challenge for society. James Anderson's new and insightful book provides a fresh perspective with respect to these challenges.

Drawing on his many years of teaching and research about teaching and learning, as well as his broad experience at levels in higher education institutions, Anderson presents a guidebook for transformational change in our institutions. However, rather than simply espousing lofty ideals, Anderson's book presents both thorough analyses of the challenges as well as practical examples and recommendations for successful implementation.

I have a personal interest in this book, because Wheaton College's strategic plan, *Wheaton 2014: Transforming Lives to Change the World*, recognizes the dual significance of diversity and globalism in a number of ways. The plan has six milestones, one of which states:

> Diversity and excellence will distinguish the Wheaton learning experience, define the Wheaton community, and delineate Wheaton's academic culture.

I have appointed a presidential action team to monitor our progress toward reaching this milestone, and to provide leadership for making excellence inclusive at Wheaton. This book will provide a broader context for understanding the urgency of the work we have ahead of us at Wheaton while at the same time providing really pragmatic approaches to these challenges. I plan to purchase a book for each member of the team.

Almost forty years ago as a senior in college, I seriously thought that higher educational institutions in particular would have learned how to use diversity as an educational asset by the year 2000. As a leader in higher education, I am profoundly disappointed and embarrassed that we are in 2007 still facing some of the elusive challenges that stymied us in the twentieth century. In fact, higher education has lagged behind almost all other institutions in this regard. This book provides me with a glimmer of hope.

The book does so because it not only objectively makes the case for making diversity and globalism the drivers of institutional mission, but maps strategies for co-opting all institutional stakeholders. Not least, James Anderson uses the concept of "intellectual diversity" as a catalyst to engage faculty in the conversation, and take ownership of the process, by *demonstrating* how diversity aligns with their disciplinary and scholarly values, and *how it* will enrich teaching, learning, and research outcomes. His approach is buttressed by an insistence that the process of change be evidence based and supported by rigorous assessment.

What is new about his vision of transformative change is the recognition that everyone in the institution, from those in academic and student affairs to the president and the trustees, can play a leadership role; he offers each constituency a clear sense of the benefits of adopting the twin values of diversity and globalism.

Ronald A. Crutcher
President, Wheaton College
Wheaton, Ohio

INTRODUCTION

One of the most exciting, yet challenging dynamics occurring at colleges and universities involves applying reengineering processes to increase levels of excellence and transformation. For some campuses such actions point to a desire to maintain their competitive edge with their peer institutions in terms of national rankings. Other campus leaders are targeting economic and environmental sustainability. A smaller but emerging group of leaders is marketing its members as 21st-century institutions in response to various forces. For example, shifting demographics have convinced many campuses to enhance their institutional capacity for diverse populations. Global workforce needs have motivated some faculties to incorporate global competencies into their academic curricula; rapidly changing technology has required students to become more technologically literate; and legal and political dynamics and societal needs translate into educating our students to become citizens and leaders who can and should shape positive outcomes for society. Even when they are addressed, the aforementioned realities generally do not reshape the culture of our campuses because they don't translate easily into the language of the academy, nor do they affect its fundamental values.

The readiness of a college or university to confront its 21st-century responsibilities is directly correlated with the degree to which it has embedded diversity and globalism concerns into the basic philosophy and infrastructure of the institution. In this context this book attempts to frame the challenges and considerations that administrative leaders, faculty, trustees, and others who shape the vision and direction of the institution must address. I start from the premise that there is a distinct difference between an institution's mission and vision statement about diversity and globalism, and its clear articulation of goals, objectives, and outcomes about diversity in a learning-centered context. No matter how well they are written, the mission and vision statement by themselves are conceptual in nature and cannot motivate an institution to change. Many campus leaders steadfastly proclaim their support for increasing diversity or "representativeness" in the student body and among faculty. The reality, however, is that attending solely to demographic concerns does not require an examination of the academic mission, the infrastructure that supports it, the definition of excellence, or the quality of leaders who do not fully comprehend the challenges associated with reculturing the academy.

Leadership strategies for advancing campus diversity may vary somewhat because they must fit into different campus frameworks and address different institutional needs. The one constant is that transformational leadership invariably must account for the very challenges that frequently hinder incorporation of diversity and globalism within the academy.

Among the critical challenges that campus leaders must confront and address are the following:

- Creating within the university community a sense of obligation for and commitment to blending two critically important ideals: the maintenance of meritocracy and the pursuit of egalitarian ideals (diversity, affirmative action, and globalism). The unsubstantiated belief on many campuses is that these two principles contradict one another, and that one—meritocracy—is more reflective of the mission statement than the other. Dr. William M. Chace, the former president of Emory University, captures the essence of this challenge when he states: "[T]he meritocratic ethos of a campus, no matter how determined and spirited, cannot afford to be unreflective of the social realities defining the United States. That way lies a form of university life that is abstract, rootless, and 'academic' in the worst sense. Intellectual rigor turns out to be no rigor at all, if established in an atmosphere purged of social reality." (1998, p. 120)
- Promoting an effective balance between two strategic approaches that address diversity concerns: deductive and inductive. Deductive approaches and solutions to diversity start from something general (i.e., demographic diversity, the moral imperative associated with affirmative action, campus incidents, campus programming, salary inequities, etc.) and build a case to support the issue. An inductive approach asks

members of the campus community to construct their ideas about diversity from varied sources of information and to link them to fundamental themes, values, or structures. The inductive approach relies on modes of inquiry (reflection, analysis, and evaluation) that are more likely to lead to integration within the academy. The challenge for campus leaders is to avoid being seduced by generic strategies that cannot promote concrete outcomes because they do not require an introspective analysis of the institution.

- Evaluating the evidence the institution offers to demonstrate that it really does produce graduates who possess 21st-century competencies. Such data help to concretize the multiple meanings and assumptions that are attributed to diversity and globalism, and they direct campus energies toward the achievement of such institutional outcomes producing global citizens among its graduates. Campus leaders who do not exhibit evidence-based and data-driven decision making should be asked to confirm the validity of those strategies they select to promote the diversity agenda.

- Understanding that the application of a scholarly approach to teaching, learning, and research can equally apply to diversity. Absence of an emphasis on the "scholarship of diversity" limits the opportunities for students to understand the role diversity and globalism can play in their overall educational experience. Faculty may not be motivated to explore the added value of curricular and pedagogical transformation simply because they are unaware of best practices and models of excellence, or, as a community of faculty, they have not forged an ethical commitment to a community of diverse learners.

Colleges and universities evolve each day, but the truth is that very few institutions take the time to face their fundamental challenges, especially those that demand us to ask hard questions about difficult areas. Campus leaders cannot back away from this responsibility, and they should be held accountable when they choose to do so. This book can be considered as both a range of considerations and examples, and as a continuum, with minimal responsibility at one end and maximum effectiveness at the other. As the author I make blunt statements about the responsibilities of certain positions, such as chief academic officer, because of the leverage that individuals in these positions exercise, and because their involvement or noninvolvement alters the academic landscape. The commitment to building an institutional model for student success, faculty excellence, and diversity begins with transformational leadership and matures into a contract of ownership involving all members of the community.

I begin this volume by creating the theoretical framework for identifying the important questions, placing the diversity discussion into a learning-centered context, and then charging institutional leaders with the responsibility for organizational change. Following that introduction my emphasis moves to faculty perspectives on diversity, the teaching and learning paradigm, diversifying or transforming the curriculum, and empowering the voice of diverse students. A common thread across the chapters is my belief that the most substantive, long-term change will occur when diversity and globalism are linked strategically to teaching and learning outcomes. The reader should note a significant amount of complementarity across chapters in the same way that learning appears to be linked throughout the undergraduate and graduate experience. In a way, this book represents a call for better assessment and more thorough documentation not only of our traditional teaching, learning, and student engagement outcomes, but also of our institutional belief that we are laboratories of preparation for the 21st century.

Faculty and their work receive a disproportionate amount of attention because the discussion about diversity and its place in the academy cannot occur without considering the classroom, academic discipline, research, and teaching and learning—period. There is no wiggle room on this one. Faculties generally are familiar with the norms for discourse in their respective disciplines and, to a lesser degree, those about teaching. Yet, even in the most traditional disciplines, students should have the opportunity for diverse experiences and for linking those experiences to their academic training. Many faculty are just beginning to learn and understand how diversity can elevate the quality of teaching, their research agendas, and their interactions with students and with one another. Systematic use of active and collaborative pedagogies is a key element inside and outside the classroom in fostering effective student learning.

The goal of this book is to challenge institutional leaders to become a visible presence in the next level of discourse about diversity that builds on previous efforts but represents a more complex set of issues and questions. How do we know that the learning and social environment of a campus prepares its students to challenge stereotypes, or become good citizens in a pluralistic society, or develop the necessary skills and competencies to work effectively with colleagues from diverse backgrounds? In terms of intellectual outcomes, we may ask: Do our diversity efforts in the discipline produce students with highly developed relational abilities and deep critical thinking skills? Those campuses that exhibit consistent caution or visible fear about engaging their community in the critical discourse on diversity and globalism contradict the very mission statement that underscores their existence. Moreover, their public statements about institutional excellence and quality must be reexamined in light of the inescapable demands of the 21st century. This is especially true for those institutions with long and prominent historical legacies that simultaneously represent strengths and weaknesses, and sometimes use the former to camouflage one of the most glaring shortcomings—lack of a viable institutional commitment to diversity.

The notion of diversity enrichment represents a range of activities on campuses, including such traditional concerns as affirmative action recruiting and hiring, diversity programming, community building, etc., but such considerations are no longer sufficient. Again, my contention is twofold:

- transformational and structural change must be driven by assertive and proactive leadership that is accountable, and
- when conjoined with more traditional academic and co-curricular outcomes, diversity outcomes are more powerful in supporting the vision of a learning-centered institution. That is, after all, how excellence and the competitive edge will be defined in the 21st century.

The blueprint institutional leaders can use should be extensive because of the challenging nature of applying transformative strategies. With this in mind, this book joins other bodies of work with a similar goal. Together they can inform and empower those who are charged with advancing the mission of teaching and learning and student development. An engaged campus community that embraces diversity and globalism truly understands the road to excellence in the 21st century.

Those colleges and universities that assertively pursue educational excellence are best served by administrative officers and faculty leaders who understand the forces that pressure organizations to change and who exhibit the characteristics associated with transformational leadership. Concerning the often difficult discussions about applying diversity and globalism, such leaders are willing to lead candid conversations about the presence or absence of concrete diversity outcomes within the fundamental structures and processes that underscore the educational mission. They often apply a critical lens to those areas that can have a broad and pervasive impact as they encourage others to promote the relationship among diversity/globalism, academic excellence, and a positive institutional climate.

Tentative leadership ultimately extracts a cost for educational institutions in terms of organizational effectiveness, reputation, and attainment of promises made to various constituents. Campus leaders would appear to be hard-pressed to rally support for a vision of 21st-century excellence that does not embrace diversity and globalism in concrete and affirmative ways, and that does not permeate some of the institution's most important academic considerations and values. This book seeks to assist those leaders who embrace the challenge of transformational change and continued educational excellence.

References

Chace, W. M. (1998, January). The pursuit of meritocratic and egalitarian ideals on college campuses. *Black Issues in Higher Education*, p. 120.

I

DEFINING DIVERSITY IN LEARNING-CENTERED CONTEXTS

Within the American higher education system, perhaps no issue has been discussed and debated more in the last two decades than diversity. Despite the intellectual grounding of equity that underscores the mission and vision of colleges and universities and the opportunity to exhibit transformational leadership, institutions and their leaders often struggle to successfully address the seemingly complex concept of diversity.

At a very general and simplistic level, a discussion about diversity could begin with the following three issues:

- **Planning issue** refers to the ways an institution conceptualizes diversity and its relationship to the mission, vision, and strategic plan.
- **Process issue** refers to the established systems, procedures, and practices used to institute, develop, and manage diversity.
- **Person issue** refers to the context and quality of the interactions that occur as people who are diverse engage one another at all levels of the institution.

Although it is possible to emphasize any one issue, the best opportunity for successfully integrating diversity rests in an institution's ability to engage in cross-sectional activities. The fundamental assumption is that critical issues, processes, and personal outcomes are intertwined in a synergistic relationship.

While it is important to question the extent to which diversity has become broadly and deeply institutionalized in American higher education, it is more productive and valuable to demonstrate individual institutional commitment, especially at the levels that effect change in students' values, development, and learning. Since colleges and universities vary in terms of their character, processes, and practices, it follows that indicators of commitment to diversity will also vary, even when they are assigned higher institutional priority.

Since many institutions use their mission statements as public pronouncements of their core values, they have the opportunity to provide a general framework to express and, ultimately, integrate diversity beliefs and values. The emphasis is that, at least, this opportunity represents a triggering mechanism, even in the absence of evidence of integration, implementation, and institutionalization of diversity. A common assumption is that most institutions use a mission, vision, or goal statement to endorse diversity, yet the reality is that such proclamations do not translate into real change, nor do they remove institutional barriers. In other words, diversity continues to be a difficult discussion if one assumes that broad university statements can have an impact in the absence of a commitment to more fundamental organizational change. Such an assumption can also indicate institutional naiveté on the part of its leadership.

Diversity as a Difficult Discussion

Campus communities regularly engage in conversations about enrollment planning, curricular change, faculty development, student leadership, human resources, athletics, research, etc. Yet, these same campuses fail, or at least struggle, to resolve the critical dialogue about diversity. This does not imply that campus efforts are stagnant, rather, while diversity activities seem to be present, their impact seems short term and their efficacy difficult to assess. Many of these activities cannot, by their very nature, address long-term systemic concerns.

The roadblocks below hinder lucid, objective, and goal-oriented discussions about diversity in the seminal stages of a campus conversation.

Lack of Clarity and Focus

Has there been a consensus and agreement on the definition (institutional) of diversity that a campus presents to the public, and on the definition (contextual) that different groups would apply under appropriate conditions? Have institutional leaders identified the locus of emphasis: policies, regulations, practices (formal and informal), planning documents/activities, and student and/or faculty outcomes? Is the focus consistent until a particular diversity outcome is completed? Do internal and external stakeholders share the same perceptions? If they do not, how reliable are the modes of communication used with traditional topics or initiatives when the effort addresses nontraditional areas such as diversity? Which campus leaders are charged with sustaining the focus, and which ones assume that responsibility? Are campus leaders clear on the modes of evaluation that will apply to their diversity responsibilities as opposed to their more traditional ones?

A lack of clarity and focus can dissipate energy and result in loss of morale. Surface efforts substitute for substance, short-term activities masquerade as long-term outcomes, and strategic thinking about diversity becomes an exercise in futility. Also, diversity detractors and nonsupporters can capitalize on environments that are rife with vague definitions and messages. Even the most committed leaders can unknowingly create the conditions that limit the progress and implementation of diversity goals.

Need for a Conceptual Model

The political and moral imperatives that often underscore leadership decisions about diversity can also preclude the development of a conceptual model that would promote broader buy-in by campus constituencies. This assertion does not devalue the importance of accounting for political, historical, and/or moral factors in the pursuit of diversity goals. In fact, such factors often serve as the catalysts that move institutions to embrace the challenges and opportunities associated with a serious consideration of diversity. Yet, most colleges and universities do not discuss diversity outside of a consistent number of targeted domains, among them:

- affirmative action;
- increasing the presence of underrepresented groups;
- promoting a welcoming environment;
- activities associated with multiculturalism;
- inequities (salary, hiring, etc.);
- admissions considerations; and
- curricular initiatives (on a limited scale).

The degree to which these areas or domains promote institutional transformation is directly linked to their conceptual, strategic, and practical connections to important areas of operational functioning. If there is no formal written diversity plan, what is linked to the college/university strategic plan? To what degree are diversity efforts or initiatives part of the charge of regular work of the most influential campus committees? How does diversity influence the emphasis on assessment of teaching and learning outcomes or a philosophy of striving to become a learning-centered campus? How are diversity considerations incorporated into the evaluation process for administrative leaders?

Finally, among the target domains that campuses emphasize, what are their conceptual links, and what evidence is there that the linkages make a real difference? Does a plan for hiring underrepresented faculty include planning to diversify the curriculum? If a decision is made to reconcile salary inequities for women, how will this affect resource decisions for other targeted diversity initiatives? The most effective leadership decisions about diversity should be grounded in a sound conceptual framework that reflects best models, practices, and research. Early discussions and the ultimate approval of a conceptual model should encourage public interaction with varied groups and a consensus among a significant number of them.

Lack of Administrative Leadership

Among the array of theories and ideas about leadership in higher education, few have emerged that connect the transformational leadership that genuinely promotes organizational change with diversity. To do so would imply that one facilitates the other, and that diversity represents a significant factor in how an institution sees itself, conducts its business, and ultimately documents where it wants to go. Normally, change is slow and developmental in any organization. Change that is prompted by diversity can often paralyze leadership and the attendant decisions that are necessary to support diversity and institutional excellence.

Some of the most effective administrative leaders, whose decisions affect traditional areas, may be unaware of the core diversity challenges they confront. They may not expect regular accountability reports, so information about diversity does not move up the line. The campus politics associated with diversity (real or perceived) can further entrench those leaders who exhibit a risk-averse leadership style or move others to consider (potential) negative consequences that eventually carry more weight more during critical decisions. The dynamics associated with administrative leadership at colleges and universities can be powerful and complex. There is more than a subtle difference between leaders who manage well and those who also take well-informed risks. Transformational leadership demands both and is necessary for diversity to become an integral part of the educational structure. Table 1.1 presents an integrative comparison across three types of leadership, all of which inform transformational leadership.

While each type of leadership can be perceived as a focal anchor that can drive a campus's agenda, the reality is that transformational leadership seeks to incorporate both an evidentiary basis for decision making (responsibility-centered) and an institutional emphasis on mission and values.

It is quite common to think of leadership as being embodied in a key person or a few key people within an organization or institution. While a formal organizational chart can locate individuals within a hierarchy of roles, positions, and responsibilities, it says little about the purpose and productivity

TABLE 1.1
Leadership

	Transformational	*Responsibility-Centered*	*Values-Based*
Focus	Changing Culture	Accountability	Mission & Vision
Challenge	Traditional barriers • Policies • Practices • Organizations	• Resource limitations • Fears of accountability	• Lack of vision • Politics • Lack mechanisms for infusion
Supplemental Factors (Catalysts)	• Presence of existing initiatives • Trusted leadership	• Pressures for accountability • Prior evidence of success	• Committed opinion leaders • Interface with planning process
Assessment	Descriptive Quantitative/ Qualitative	Quantitative/ Objective	Qualitative/ Affective

of the "leadership team." It is within the team that a continuity of thinking, planning, and commitment emerges.

In the case of developing a diverse campus community, it is vital that organizational efforts be perceived as evolving from the activities of leadership teams and not just from those of individuals. Page (2003) suggests that a leadership team will be committed to five key features in the production of a diversity community:

1. A commitment to understanding other cultures and the value of diversity in leadership positions
2. The understanding and commitment to basic values that flow through the organization
3. The creation of a culture of trust where the diverse organization respects all of the cultures it includes
4. The conscious development of strategies to recruit and/or provide mobility for women and ethnic minorities within the organization
5. A willingness to be accountable for the success or failure of promoting diversity within the academic leadership and for monitoring and mentoring the leaders

Although it may be self-evident, the first building block on which an institution can promote diversity is to employ leaders who recognize that they must serve all constituents to secure followers from any constituency—this is the core of servant leadership, one of the most powerful and useful theories of leadership that supports a diversity culture (Greenleaf, 1970). If the effective inclusion of diversity has the potential and power to transform institutional climates, then transformative leadership must be present to embed diversity into the college and university culture and to establish an institutional framework for accountability.

Public Expectations of Leadership: A "Snapshot" of Diversity and Academic Excellence

Unless an executive leader (chief executive officer and chief administrative officer in particular) is able to generate a comprehensive conceptual model of diversity in a relatively short period, the evolution of a strong vision and model will take approximately 18 months to two years. This allows for an introduction, a broad review, community feedback, a second iteration, and public acceptance. In the interim and thereafter, it would benefit the campus community to receive updated reports on the institution's progress toward diversity goals. A diversity scorecard would have more value when presented in the context of other important indicators. For example, it could be represented as shown below.

While the indicators shown below have individual value for both ongoing (formative) assessment and outcomes-related (summative) assessment, it is their integrative relationship that embellishes an institution's comments about excellence and effectiveness. For example, an internal leadership deci-

Diversity and Institutional Excellence Scorecard

- Indicators of Impact of Diversity on Traditional Outcomes Associated with Institutional Effectiveness (for example, participation with members of other races in academic courses prepares student to function effectively in a global society)
- Indicators That Diversity Is Affected by Institutional Policies and Practices (for example, the effects of race-neutral admissions policies on minority college enrollment)
- Indicators of Institutional Effectiveness (for example, reduction in first- to second-semester attrition among first-generation and low-income students)
- Indicators of Program Effectiveness (for example, regular participation in tutorial sessions reduces differential grade performance across student groups)
- Indicators of Student Learning and Intellectual Growth (for example, campus leaders exhibit greater maturity in decision-making skills after exposure to diversity training)
- Indicators of Student Academic/Social Integration (for example, students voluntarily increase their participation in study groups with students of different races)
- Indicators of Student Success/Achievement (for example, a consistent increase over three years in the number of Hispanic students who compete for national fellowships)
- Indicators of Reputational Enhancement (for example, young Ph.D.s select an institution for employment and one incentive is the earlier success of current female faculty)
- Indicators of an Enhanced Climate and/or Community (for example, a consistent increase in the number of majority students who enroll in African studies courses)

sion can lead to the recruitment and matriculation of a select community of diverse learners. Those students can then participate in a program that encourages dynamic engagement and incremental gains in academic self-esteem. The program can be identified as a national benchmark for academic success and achievement and can enhance the institution's national reputation.

Disconnect with Faculty Work and Academic Initiatives

Many faculty are not convinced that diversity represents a sound investment in the academic culture. Such an investment would need to be related to their intrinsic and extrinsic values, to faculty productivity and sustainability, and to the mission of the academic department. When diversity is not a part of regular conversations among faculty, it does not emerge on their radar screen, and it does not receive the support of the most important campus constituency.

How, then, can we present faculty with a best-case scenario on diversity that will encourage their investment and involvement? Perhaps campuses need to shift their attention from an overinvestment in short-term program activities (that primarily reside in student affairs) to proposed long-term projects that influence academic collaborations and are the result of faculty work. While it is true that faculty may respond to diversity-related incentives, it is also true that they must respond to real-world challenges such as the increasing presence of ethnically, socially, economically, and linguistically diverse students. How can institutions advance their educational goals when faculty do not acknowledge the demands of preparing all students for 21st-century realities? What happens to a curriculum and the pedagogy when faculty do not claim ownership for diversity? If faculty accept the charge of remaining on the cutting edge of institutional quality, then they should accept those aspects of diversity that are inextricable components of quality as well. Which incentives associated with diversity engagement attract younger junior faculty, and which ones appeal to senior faculty and to researchers?

Developing a Culture of Evidence

During the last two decades, colleges and universities have developed and supported a number of diversity-related projects and initiatives. This support has been sponsored by higher education associations, private and corporate foundations, state systems, community organizations, and individual donors. This is often in addition to the investment that individual campuses make. What difference has all this activity made?

It is difficult to give a general answer since such an assessment requires a similarity of scale, format, and institutional type. Each institution, however, is responsible for demonstrating the quality and effectiveness of traditional and nontraditional programs, including those associated with diversity. Why do so many campuses fall short in assessing the efficacy of their diversity efforts? I address this question in depth later, but, generally speaking, institutions that are not committed to outcomes assessment do not seek to develop a culture of evidence to support diversity.

Without a body of evidence that demonstrates an impact, diversity investments can be challenged, leadership decisions can be questioned, and effective planning is hampered. Thus, assessment plans must become a fundamental aspect of the fabric that underscores institutional support for diversity. A commitment to assessment initiates a planning process for implementing campus diversity practices and strategies.

An example of the importance of assessment and evaluation in diversity planning and institutional transformation is the Campus Diversity Initiative (CDI), funded by the James Irvine Foundation (2000–05), which involved 28 campuses in California (AAC&U, 2007). The CDI project assisted institutions with their evaluation efforts by providing a generic analysis instrument (CDI Evaluation Project Rubric). The CDI rubric complements the comprehensive and multidimensional conceptual framework that served as an overlay for the project and its implementation on each campus.

The James Irvine Foundation also funded the Diversity Scorecard (DS) project, which represented a partnership between 14 universities, colleges, and community colleges throughout Southern California and the Center for Urban Education at the University of Southern California. The DS is an ongoing research project based on a culture of evidence model. Institutions collect and analyze diverse data on the performance of students of color and construct a framework to evaluate the information. The disaggregation of routinely collected institutional data allows campuses to identify gaps in academic performance and unearth educational inequities, thus permitting them to generate meaningful action plans (Bensimon, 2004).

The Power of Campus Myths and a Vacant Historical Chronology

To what degree are incoming students' general educational goals and expectations for college associated with diversity? Do faculty's sociopolitical attitudes affect student ideology, and, if so, how are they conveyed? How do student beliefs and attitudes affect their desire to interact with different groups across demographic categories? When student backlash to diversity occurs, what are the origins? What are the specific areas of concern for different racial and ethnic groups over time, that is, what changes and what remains static?

These questions and their answers are often associated with the preconceived notions of students about the presence and impact of diversity on society, on campus, and in their personal lives. A critical issue is that many students, and some faculty, lack the knowledge base and diverse experience that allow for objective and critical examination of diversity. This vacuum is compounded by an institution's inability to tackle myths about diversity and to move beyond soft diversity programs that have little impact on misinformation.

Institutional leaders often face the challenge of decision making without the benefit of a history and chronology of diversity efforts and their impact on their campus. They are hampered when they attempt to project diversity outcomes before implementation. Another concern is that these same leaders are less willing to take risks in a climate devoid of a historical context. A critical factor in enhancing the confidence level of leaders, the university community, and the public is to demonstrate the "educational benefits" that diversity provides to all students both past and present.

Diversity in a Learner-Centered Context

Earlier in the chapter I mentioned difficulties that arise when the diversity discussion on a campus is not underscored by a sound conceptual framework. This issue is of paramount importance in any discussion of student success and achievement and their relationship with teaching, learning and curricular outcomes. In this context, an institution, or at least the academic side, should offer a conceptualization of what is valued and/or important in a teaching-learning paradigm. For example, Anderson (2006) suggested the model in Table 1.2, which identifies an integrated relationship among areas that affect learner-centered outcomes.

TABLE 1.2
Integrated Model of Learner-Centered Education

Academic Success	Transition Into the First Year of College	Assessment and Self-Discovery
Developmental and general curriculum	Intrusive advising and mentoring	Learning styles
Academic supports	College course analysis and time management	Noncognitive and environmental factors
Study skill Assessment	Information and computer literacy	Career exploration and decision making
Test-taking skills	Cocurricular experiences	Active learning strategies
Active learning strategies		

This model becomes the backdrop for analytical discussions about incorporating diversity. For example, an analysis of a sequence of courses (second column) may indicate that a diversity of active learning strategies (first column) and learning styles (third column) may correlate positively with course grades. While this seems to be beneficial for all students, it may have even more significance for certain categories of diverse students (e.g., first-generation commuters who are older students). Without a conceptual model, such a consideration may never appear on the radar screen. A robust learner-centered model could be complemented by the development of a parallel teaching-centered model, and the presence of both would serve as a strong indicator that cultural change is emerging at the most fundamental levels of the institution.

The Contextual Case for Diversity Definitions

The remaining chapters in this volume define diversity relative to the topical discussion in each. While it is temping to offer a single, overarching definition that germinates several subdefinitions, any definition has more value when it can be applied meaningfully. Ideological diversity cannot be defined in terms of demographic diversity, although they might share a common ground. Such concepts as pluralism, cultural democracy, and multiculturalism can have varying definitions, but there is no shared consensus among a community of users of those concepts.

In discussing a particular topic, such as curricular transformation, however, an institution might want to clarify and expand the definition of diversity. Diversity as a component of a core curriculum experience can be different from or similar to diversity as a mandatory set of course requirements (for all students) that have no relationship to general education outcomes: general education outcomes are best measured relative to an undergraduate experience or a number of learning outcomes. A distributive set of diversity courses or credit hours may not be linked by a defined set of outcomes that offers insight into a shared educational experience. Another example is the metrics of counting diverse faculty (their presence) compared with evaluating the impact of their presence on student success and development. A global definition of diversity can serve a purpose within a broad mission statement or set of goals, but as we delve further down in an organization, more attention should focus on tailored operational definitions.

The difficulties associated with defining diversity can also be shared with attempts to define "community." While some researches and educators have tried to identify a common definition of community that can be applied universally to colleges and universities, others have attempted to isolate distinct characteristics that constitute a good campus community. It is possible to visualize diversity and community as being "defined" on one end of a continuum and "achieved" at the other end, with varied mediating factors affecting the processes and outcomes that exist along the continuum.

X_____X

Defining Diversity
and Community

Achieving Diversity
and Community

Mediating Factors

What has been most elusive for college campuses is identifying those institutional factors that mediate the transition from definition to achievement. McDonald (2002) suggests that the constantly changing nature of campus populations, together with the lack of an agreed-upon framework for community, exacerbates our efforts to build community on campuses. It should be evident that the evolution of both diversity and community share a common pathway of research, implementation, and, ultimately, impact. It is also reasonable that definitions, achievements, and outcomes be influenced by best research and practices, but shaped by the institutional context.

When diversity is defined as a collection of campus-based activities that encourage involvement, the degree and kind of involvement vary because the interests and commitments of individuals and groups vary. This type of involvement is optional and voluntary; moreover, it sits at the margins of the traditional academic mission, faculty work, and student learning. In this circumstance diversity is relegated to projects, special programs, short-term initiatives, and other efforts that are not sustainable and are difficult to evaluate.

On the other hand, diversity can be defined and shaped by the parameters of institutional engagement, which require strategic thinking, mission-driven activities, and recognition of values and priorities. For those campuses that wade into the unanticipated questions and implications that emerge from a commitment to diversity as a set of engagement activities, a useful frame of reference is needed. In his discussion of engagement activities, Derek Bok (1982), a former president of Harvard University, offers three important questions for assessment that can be extrapolated to an institutional consideration of diversity:

1. How important is the social (and institutional) need and how likely is it that the university will succeed in doing something about it?
2. Will the requested actions interfere with the freedom of individual professors and students, especially with their freedom to form their own beliefs and express their own opinions?
3. What new burdens (e.g., resources, time, and loss of autonomy) will the desired initiative have on the institution as a whole?

According to Bok, an institution should not embark on a new initiative without first making certain that the project commands the enthusiasm and support of faculty members, because, without widespread faculty involvement, support, and ownership, these initiatives are destined to fail. Engaged universities provide new opportunity structures, resources, and pathways for faculty and students. They also develop an infrastructure for engagement-related priorities, programs, organizational structures, and cultures (Walshok, 1999).

Incorporating a Core Identity

Most colleges and universities have developed a consensus about certain descriptive aspects of their "core ideology." These core characteristics may reflect how the institution defines itself (liberal arts, research intensive/extensive, private/public, urban, land grant, minority-serving, etc.) or whom it serves (first-generation and/or low-income students, females only, nontraditional students, commuters, top 10 percent, etc.). In many cases diversity is referenced as a primary institutional value associated with access, equity, and representation, but not with academic mission. As a result, many campus constituents (internal and external) see diversity as an important process or initiative or even goal, yet they cannot make substantive statements about the educational value of diversity or its place within the core identity/ideology.

Two important questions arise from this discussion that could inform the critical discourse about diversity at many institutions: In the absence of diversity represented as a core ideology, can an institution realistically expect transformational change and educational enhancement to occur? In the absence of diversity represented as a core ideology, what can be said about the stated core values of an institution and their impact on guiding leadership decisions?

The core ideology of an organization is composed of several characteristics: a consistent identity that transcends periodic environmental changes; a statement of purpose that articulates the organization's reason for being; the presence of core values and enduring principles; and a belief system that affirms commitment to the ideology and the institution. The call for diversity is enhanced and strengthened when diversity is incorporated as a core ideology, and doing so also necessitates a review of other organizational ideologies that often have a long, venerated history.

Introducing a core ideology on diversity, its affirmation, and its acceptance will occur in developmental phases, and campus leaders must plan their selected strategies and points of emphasis. What should not happen, though it often does, is that certain activities or initiatives related to diversity become confused with the existence of a core ideology. As noted in other chapters, senior leadership will play a central role in demystifying misconceptions about diversity and orienting/reorienting campuses to embrace a functional discussion on diversity as a core ideology.

When diversity is applied to the academic mission, it should contribute to the institution's identity as a powerful place for learning. While many factors can contribute to such an important outcome, the role of academic leadership is central to any concrete and measurable assessment of success. If the existing structural quality of undergraduate programs has not included diversity as a functional tool for self-examination, certain questions should be raised: How confident can an institution be in the development and maturity of some student competencies, especially those that are associated with the realities of the 21st century? What can be said about academic leadership that does not address the importance or role of diversity in student learning, effective teaching, program quality, and institutional effectiveness? Can we sustain faculty trust and commitment if we suggest that they build an enhanced culture of engagement and learning that is intentional and purposeful and that includes outcomes associated with diversity and globalism?

Educated Versus Uneducated Compassion

In a subsequent chapter I discuss the critical role that "learning communities" can play as vital structures that allow and encourage students to have a shared dialogue about diverse beliefs, perceptions, feelings, and experiences. Lardner (2005, p. 28) offers a succinct and more powerful description when she states, "learning communities can become places where students and teachers experience the gift of learning with others who understand the world differently not just because of disciplinary differences, but also because of genuine differences in how we experience and interpret reality, how and where we are situated, and the social identities that shape our thinking. What animates an effective learning community is a sense of our shared future, mindfulness about our responsibility to imagine a larger public good to which we can work." She suggests that an animating principle that threads the outcomes associated with diversity, educational equity, and learning communities is compassion—not viewed simply as an empathic emotion but understood more significantly as a series of cognitive processes, decisions, and judgments, of which one can become more conscious (Nussbaum, 2003).

The intellectual agendas that campuses and their faculty use as guideposts to inform students about the place of diversity in their curricular and pedagogical experiences should be portrayed as cognitive, affective, and emotional outcomes. Educated compassion involves a series of steps that can begin with exposure to academic/disciplinary content and information, which in turn frame our discussions, decisions, and judgments about the seriousness and importance of diversity that is not ours or is not part of our reality. The next step is to validate the experiences of others, both positive and negative. Finally, an understanding and acceptance of shared experiences and realities becomes coupled with empathy.

Uneducated compassion is reflected in a shallow or disingenuous attempt to understand the diverse realities of others. An incomplete or fragmented knowledge base results in faulty judgments and decision making. The inability to engage in a serious way information about the realities of others keeps us from validating their experiences and circumstances. Individuals in this category prioritize what realities should be validated and valued. For example, many White students are reluctant to register for what they perceive as "diversity courses" because they don't need them to complete their major, and because they do not perceive them as rigorous, valid, or pertinent to their own self-interest. Thus a discussion of "White privilege" and its historical and contemporary legacy for people of color becomes a nonissue for many White students; it is not part of their reality or that of their reference group. Moreover, they view the concept as a political artifact of those with unsubstantiated and/or skewed perceptions or those who push a so-called politically correct agenda.

How do we convince a larger and more diverse group of students to accept their educational experiences and achievements as an investment in 21st-century outcomes that affect them, their communities, and their country—and to recognize that these outcomes are inextricably linked to the ways that diversity and globalism are embedded into successful paradigms of teaching and learning? How should colleges and universities reconceptualize their mission and vision, expand their core identity, and reengineer their structures to facilitate the transformation that accompanies 21st-century excellence? What are the consequences for an institution and its constituents of missed opportunities for transformational change? Finally, what new demands for accountability must academic and administrative leaders embrace in their pursuit of educational equity and excellence?

The example on pages 24 and 25, on the surface, allows an observer to view one aspect of organizational dynamics. At the real heart of the matter is the responsibility of an open-admissions institution to position its mission to serve the needs of a very diverse population in the face of a rigid and authoritarian leadership style at the top that precludes broad participation and stifles creativity.

The Power of the University of Michigan Case

The future structure and direction of diversity efforts in higher education will be shaped to a significant degree by the June 2003 Supreme Court decision involving two lawsuits brought against the University of Michigan. Both cases involved the criteria associated with admissions decisions in the School of Law and the College of Literature, Science and Arts. In *Gratz v. Bollinger* the Court struck down the practice of overweighting race by assigning a set number of points to applicants. On the other hand, in *Grutter v. Bollinger*, the Court endorsed the Law School's holistic evaluation process that included race as one of many factors—an effective compromise between the proponents of merit and diversity.

While the explicit focus of each case, and the Court deliberations, was on incorporating race, other critical issues and outcomes emerged that would support the success of the *Grutter* decision and shape the future of the critical discourse on diversity. In *Defending Diversity: Affirmative Action at the University of Michigan* (Gurin, Lehman, & Lewis, 2004), those closest to the case, the university's faculty, indicated that the Supreme Court accepted the Law School's pedagogic interest in having a racially diverse student body as constitutionally compelling. Their discussion focuses on three points:

- There is a constitutional basis for giving some deference to the academic judgment of universities.
- A broad array of evidence was presented to support that educational judgment.
- Diversity incorporates not only a pedagogic interest but also an interest in democratic legitimacy.

Transformative Leadership: When Risk Slows the Process—A Community College Example

In the spring of 2005, I was invited to present a series of workshops at an urban community college. The three campuses of the college had not only grown in terms of student enrollment, but they also had become increasingly more diverse in race, ethnicity, culture, class, age, gender, and disability. The two groups that received most of my attention during my visit were senior administrators and faculty, and the thematic context involved a critical discourse on three areas: transformative leadership, diversity, and positive teaching and learning outcomes.

While each topic alone could have promoted significant engagement, my goal was to encourage participants to think about what would result from a dynamic interaction of the three at different institutional levels. The college was in a favorable position to capitalize on such a discussion because of several factors: recent development of an educational master plan; a small grant from a foundation that emphasized the enhancement of the educational environment and the submission of an application to participate in a much larger grant; an urban setting with a large pool of prospective diverse students (American ethnic minorities and international); recognition of the need to develop a "culture of evidence," that is, a stronger commitment to generating data that can be used in a meaningful way; a commitment to aligning student diversity competencies with workforce development; and a belief among some administrators and faculty that a reexamination was needed of the college's philosophy of student-centeredness and diversity.

With the aforementioned factors present, one could project that this institution, and others like it, would be positioned to provide growing or at least incremental evidence of positive outcomes associated with diversity, teaching and learning, and student retention. Moreover, a visible pattern of transformative and/or evidence-based leadership should have been evident as the primary impetus for the institution's emphasis on such outcomes.

Surprisingly, campus leaders seemed to have almost diametrically opposed perceptions about many stated outcomes of success and decision makers' willingness to address important concerns. My interaction with faculty and academic instructors suggested genuine support for implementing a "student-centered" model of success and retention. However I also perceived the presence of a risk-averse atmosphere that limited or slowed the institution's progress toward organizational change. This latter conclusion was very evident in my probing interaction with senior administrators, faculty, and other decision makers from all three campuses. In one such gathering attended by about 30 individuals, only two administrators responded to the questions I posed during a PowerPoint presentation. While their responses reflected positive assertions and/or defensive reactions, they seemed to overlook two key factors: (1) for some reason, 28 of their colleagues were completely silent, and (2) there was inconclusive evidence present to support their comments.

I would reiterate that this particular community college hovers just below the threshold of becoming a national benchmark because of the presence of the aforementioned favorable conditions. During the remainder of my visit, I asked eight persons individually about the overwhelming silence at the meeting. There was a significant amount of consensus among their responses:

- The meeting reflected the organizational imbalance in which only a small number of individuals shape the institutional image, offer public commentary, make decisions, and influence the morale of others.
- People were hesitant to make any public statements that challenged or conflicted with those of the two administrators who responded.
- Several individuals simply stated that things were not going to change, and their silence protected them from potentially precarious consequences.
- The campus would mobilize for excellence under an inclusive model of transformative leadership, teaching and learning, and diversity if there was an opportunity to do so.
- Despite the risk-averse behaviors the small core group exhibited, many others respected their competence and their contributions to the institution.
- While all realized the importance of addressing diversity, their differences reflected a lack of consensus about the efficacy of strategic initiatives.

The University of Michigan accepted the responsibility of demonstrating the educational value of diversity, and providing the research evidence to support its case. Few institutions of higher education would argue with the statement that they have responsibility to (1) create the optimal learning environment that enriches the intellectual, personal, and social lives of their students; (2) contribute to the development of the values of social ethics and civic responsibility; and (3) prepare their students to function effectively in a pluralistic society and compete in a global workforce. Yet, colleges and universities vary in the degree to which they can demonstrate that the aforementioned "educational benefits" actually occur, especially those that have a relationship with diversity goals and objectives.

The research paradigm the university used was the Michigan Student Study (MSS). This project represented a very robust survey design, explored major concepts, and examined equity and institutional issues and administrative and academic collaborations. Four critical questions framed the parameters of the study:

1. How relevant is the University of Michigan's commitment to multiculturalism and diversity of its students?
2. How can institutional efforts toward multiculturalism reinforce and improve the overall educational experience of undergraduate students?
3. Can the University of Michigan's efforts improve the intellectual development and educational preparedness of our students?
4. What is the degree of racial tension on campus?
    - How much of that tension is a result of characteristics that students bring to the campus?
    - How much tension is a result of the campus climate?
    - What are the specific areas of concern about diversity issues for different racial and ethnic groups?

While the public perception of the Supreme Court case may be that the University of Michigan sought to justify its use of racial preferences in admissions decisions, the reality is that the university used longitudinal research to document the impact of diverse experiences on the educational experiences and intellectual development of *all* students. This fact is evident when one examines the major and subtopics of analysis:

- Student characteristics (expectations for college, educational goals, high school experiences, psychological/social factors, etc.)
- Student academic and social experiences on campus
- Student experiences with diversity on campus
- Student ideology and sociopolitical attitudes

The assessments were administered at student entry; at the end of the first, second, third, and fourth year; and eight years after graduation.

If it is true that the burden of proof has shifted from affirmative action and access to measures of diversity and learning outcomes, then colleges and universities cannot afford to be ill-prepared when asked to demonstrate the presence and impact of a "culture of evidence and accountability" regarding diversity. Documentation of the educational benefits of diversity in higher education can no longer be treated as a by-product of the increased presence of underrepresented groups or the added value of diversity-related activities on campus. Institutions must delineate the educational ends that diversity will facilitate and produce. The commitment, resources, expertise, and institutional will of the University of Michigan sustained it in its historic legal battle to defend its right to define the educational landscape that it associates with educational excellence.

This same challenge confronts all other two- and four-year institutions in different and, sometimes, fundamentally similar ways. Some will continue to pursue and embrace this challenge, some will struggle to find their way, and others will abandon the responsibility for inclusive and transformative leadership. This journey as much as any other will define the future of that institution.

While the Supreme Court affirmed the limited use of race in higher education to promote the educational benefits of diversity in the *Grutter v. Bollinger* decision, a more recent decision (July 2007) suggests that four-year institutions must continue to pay close attention to the goals and rationale that are offered to support diversity policies, programs, and strategies. In a 5–4 decision, the U.S. Supreme Court ruled that race cannot be used as a primary factor in student-assignment policies by the Seattle, Washington and Louisville, Kentucky school districts (*Parents Involved in Community Schools v. Seattle School District No. 1* and *Meredith v. Jefferson County Board of Education*). The chief justices sought to distinguish the school district case from the higher education decision in *Grutter*; however, the language in the majority opinion suggests that the court may be moving toward a colorblind philosophy and perhaps an unwillingness to incorporate race as a factor in all educational decisions (Bell, 2007).

The Role of Higher Education Organizations

American colleges and universities have exhibited varying levels of commitment to developing inclusive communities and their mission-based statements of support for diversity. In many instances, even when diversity becomes an integral part of the institution, its impact is localized to the campus and surrounding community. Unless there is communication with other institutions, both nationally or within the same state, the equation for success may go unnoticed or not be shared in its entirety. National higher education organizations can serve as the vehicle that links diversity conversations, provides a common language, supports persuasive research, and connects the educational discourse on diversity to broader community considerations.

Four organizations that have forged and sustained a beachhead for diversity in the higher education community and public consciousness are the American Council on Education (ACE), the recently dissolved American Association for Higher Education (AAHE), the Association of American Colleges and Universities (AAC&U), and the National Association of Student Personnel Administrators (NASPA). It is difficult to accept where we would have been during the last three decades of commitment without the efforts of those who have shaped the vision, structure, and platforms of these organizations. I can trace my own professional development as an administrator, faculty member, and scholar to the nurturing that I received from each of these organizations. The same can be said of many of my colleagues who are members of underrepresented and majority groups.

In addition to their commitment to diversity ACE, AAHE, AAC&U, and NASPA have affected leadership development, public policy discussions, assessment, lifelong learning, curricular development, teaching and learning initiatives, civic engagement, and liberal education. On June 23, 2004,

AAC&U, in cooperation with 30 higher education associations, issued a statement on "Diversity and Democracy: The Unfinished Work." This statement embraces an expanded role for higher education in its pursuit of inclusion and civic commitment. The strength of the statement, which also reflects the core commitment of AAC&U, is its focus on educational outcomes and intellectual development. Three broad components of the statement embody this emphasis:

- to work in partnership with primary and secondary educators to improve the quality of educational outcomes for poor children and children of color;
- to redouble efforts to ensure that all who enroll in college, whatever their background, experience a rigorous, horizon-expanding, and intellectually challenging education; and
- to allow every student to learn about the struggles for full inclusion in our democracy that have been a crucial part of our nation's history.

Higher education organizations have not backed away from their commitment to affirmative strategies that promote educational excellence and equity, but they have sharpened their focus to recognize the long-term value of an outcomes-based focus grounded in research, curricular change, and intellectual development. In the 21st century, diversity has evolved from a primary affirmative action goal of access and redress for past wrongdoing to a goal of broader teaching, learning, and research outcomes that have a more comprehensive impact on the academy and in society.

The presence of a strong conceptual model speaks to the degree to which an institution identifies itself as a holistic learning environment. The AAC&U conducted a study (2004) that examined the degree to which diversity was institutionalized across colleges and universities in the state of New Jersey. Of particular interest was the degree of balance between macro and micro diversity efforts on a given campus—an interaction model, compared to the more typical static analysis. The conceptual value of this model was embedded in the introduction of three measures that determined the extent of balance: centrality (macro efforts associated with institutional leadership and supportive infrastructures); pervasiveness (micro efforts at all levels); and integration (the degree to which macro and micro efforts work together). The study revealed that these measures can predict the educational quality of combined diversity initiatives as a whole, institutional sustainability, and academic excellence (Knox, 2005).

Diversity's Role in Nurturing Success

While students may graduate without embracing diversity and globalism as important aspects of their educational experience and lifelong learning, a definition of real student success encompasses a range of diverse factors. What does student success mean? France A. Cordova (2006), chancellor of the University of California, Riverside, offers an excellent definition:

> The challenge is about throughput (will a student graduate?), education (will a student learn?), career preparation (will a student acquire skills and interest for a career?), and inspiration (will a student find passion, challenge world views, and learn to value different cultures and perspectives?). It is about our future (will enough students go into science and technology fields?), our competitiveness (are foreign students better prepared?), and what we want our society to be (will our students be inspired to contribute to our culture, to shepherd our fragile environment, to give back to those who are less fortunate?). (p. 16)

She also makes two important recommendations: (1) universities should amend the curriculum, especially when it is inflexible and outdated, to be more attuned to the backgrounds and experiences of our new and diverse student body, and (2) we need to ask students and alumni questions that inform instruction (Were you challenged to think and invent? Were you challenged to link knowledge across disciplines? Were you challenged to question commonly held views? Were you challenged to envision a different future from the one you imagined as an entering student? Bold and successful presidencies are characterized by leaders who ask and answer difficult questions, and who recognize when our discussions about quality and excellence should be couched in a 21st-century context.

The Ball and Chain of Anti-Intellectual and Antidiversity Beliefs

One of the most powerful and persuasive arguments by advocates for far-reaching change for a 21st-century college education is contained in the publication, *College Learning for the New Global Century* (AAC&U, 2007). This national report represents the sustained and collective work of the LEAP (Liberal Education and America's Promise) National Council in conjunction with other advisers and leaders at the national and state levels. The AAC&U has long been a driving force for renewed excellence in higher education among educational associations and is overseeing the 10-year LEAP initiative (2005–2015).

College Learning for the New Global Century urges a new compact between educators and American society that will define liberal education for the 21st century while accounting for how scientific and technological innovation, global interdependence, cross-cultural encounters, and changes in the balance of economic and political power are reshaping the world. The power of the document is twofold: it redefines liberal education for the 21st century as a comprehensive set of goals and outcomes that are essential to the education of all students across all fields of study, and it establishes a set of standards, the Principles of Excellence, that will guide educational reform and renewal for decades to come.

In its call to leadership and action, the report affirms the critical relationship between educational excellence and the inclusion of knowledge and practices associated with diversity and globalism. Without representing any political position, the report assumes the higher ground in establishing a framework for excellence that also accounts for social, economic, and political realities. The recognition that learning is the essential goal invites using multiple pathways that faculty and students can explore as they engage big questions and apply learning to complex problems—problems they will encounter in college, work, and life.

Why, then, would some be critical of such a pragmatic, purposeful, and comprehensive approach to educational reform and educational excellence, and why would they target diversity and globalism as anti-intellectual biases that underscore a political self interest?

David Horowitz's Academic Bill of Rights and the National Association of Scholars' recommendations have encouraged institutions, state systems and councils, and legislators to ensure that colleges and universities support robust intellectual debates in and out of the classroom while limiting misunderstanding, harassment, or intimidation. Few in the academy would argue against such a laudable and time-honored tradition, and credit should be given to those who wave this banner. Unfortunately, those in the academy who champion this same outcome under the auspices of the "scholarship of diversity" have been accused unfairly of abdicating their responsibility to promote intellectual diversity.

Varied intellectual presentations about diversity that encourage reflection are not challenges to academic freedom and are not exemplars of academic unprofessionalism. Issues of power and privilege, no matter whom they point to, will always be a part of sociological, economic, and political considerations. Cross-cultural technology transfer is a 21st-century reality that must account for global cultural differences. This is far removed form Horowitz's self-described model for academic freedom—Columbia University in the late 1950s, an institution, which at that time reflected neither diversity nor globalism (quite different from today). Horowitz's conceptual framework for intellectual diversity has been translated into a formalized academic bill of rights and has been submitted as a House bill or resolution to a number of state legislatures. (Legislative action on these bills can be tracked at http://www.freeexchangeoncampus.org.) In most states the bills seek to establish balance, primarily in the classroom, among what are perceived to be liberal and conservative ideologies, beliefs, and coverage of academic content. In some states legislators representing a range of political perspectives have rejected Horowitz's fundamental contention that liberal ideologies are indoctrinating students before they have the opportunity to examine other more conservative positions. The academic bill of rights has either died in committee or been rejected in Georgia, Kentucky, Missouri, Montana, Oregon, Virginia, and West Virginia. The bill is being considered in Arizona, Massachusetts, and Montana (a new bill was submitted). It is important to note that on virtually all of the campuses examined, only a small number of students reported indoctrination or an imbalance, and these students were often members of conservative campus organizations. A larger number of faculty have shown support for Horowitz's position, but they have generally been unable to generate concrete evidence to support the conservative agenda on intellectual diversity.

Attempts to engage in debate about academic freedom and intellectual diversity should continue, since freedom of expression is a cornerstone of intellectual pursuits (Hall, 2005). However, as John Cavanaugh (2006), president of the University of West Florida, suggests, it is time to move this debate along. Along to what?—to comprehensive discussions about student success, teaching effectiveness, curricular transformation, global competitiveness, research excellence, faculty and staff development, commitment to community development, economic development, environmental sustainability, etc. We should expend our energies on supporting institutional needs as they create the 21st-century renaissance learner, not on decrying the extreme behaviors of an isolated number of faculty.

Incorporating diversity into the teaching and learning paradigm and as a core aspect of curricular transformation presupposes the student and the instructor assuming responsibility for doing so. Faculty are charged with building students' capacities to form their own evaluations about complex and controversial issues and questions. Moreover, faculty must exhibit a willingness to teach "all sides of the debate" and help students learn to engage differences of opinion, evaluate evidence, and form their own educated judgments about the relative value of competing perspectives (AAC&U, 2007). Students must exhibit a parallel appreciation for intellectual diversity—new knowledge, different perspectives, competing ideas, and alternative claims of truth, and they must pursue truth and wisdom by following the intellectual methods that will lead them to valid conclusions. And all of this must be done in the context of academic honesty.

I have often said that it is unfortunate that the diversity discussion in higher education has been reduced primarily to a discussion of demographics, politics and political correctness, recruitment and retention, and the results of climate scans and surveys. While these are important considerations, two others pertain to far wider audiences and offer the opportunity for far greater impact: (1) intellectual diversity and (2) the diversity of skill levels, learning styles, and cognitive frameworks in any given student body and between one or more student groups (undergraduate and graduate). Any definition of a scholarly community must account for these two areas of diversity in delineating the quality of scholarship and the excellence associated with teaching, learning, and curricular development. Although I do pay some attention to other important factors, it is the last two I emphasize in this book. The larger discussion about diversity should never be so fragmented that we lose its essential relationship to educational responsibility, academic quality, and the promotion of the greater good.

The rest of this book supports the fundamental position that diversity must be couched within a context of institutional engagement, be driven by transformational leadership, be valued by the faculty community, and be experienced by all students as a core component of their educational experience. We owe nothing less to those who invest in our higher educational institutions than to offer the opportunity to become 21st-century renaissance learners.

References

Association of American Colleges and Universities (AAC&U). (2007). *College learning for the new global century. A report from the National Leadership Council for Liberal Education and America's Promise.* Washington, DC: Author.

Anderson, J. A. (2006). Keynote presentation at the Annual Conference of the National Association of Developmental Education, Philadelphia, PA.

Bell, D. (2007, July 13). Desegregation's demise. *The Chronicle of Higher Education Review*, section B, p. 11.

Bensimon, E. M. (2004). The diversity scorecard: A learning approach to institutional change. *Change, 36*(1), 45–52.

Bok, D. (1982). *Beyond the ivory tower: Social responsibilities of the modern university.* Cambridge, MA: Harvard University Press.

Cavanaugh, J. C. (2006). It's time to move the academic freedom debate along. *The Presidency, 9*(2), 26.

Chace, W. M. (1998, January). The pursuit of meritocratic and egalitarian ideals on college campuses. *Black Issues in Higher Education*, p. 120.

Cordova, F. A. (2006). Losing sleep over student success. *The Presidency, 9*(2), 14–21.

Greenleaf, R. (1970). *Servant as leader.* Indianapolis, IN: Robert K. Greenleaf Center for Servant Leadership.

Gurin, P., Lehman, J. S., & Lewis, E. (2004). Defending diversity: Affirmative action at the University of Michigan. Ann Arbor: University of Michigan Press.

Hall, K. L. (2005). A cautionary tale of academic rights and responsibilities. *The Presidency, 8*(3), 22–27.

Knox, M. (2005). Institutional models that cultivate comprehensive change. *Diversity Digest, 9*(2), 10–11.

Lardner, E. (2005). *Diversity, educational equity, and learning communities.* Olympia, WA: Washington Center for Improving the Quality of Undergraduate Education, Evergreen State College.

McDonald, W. M. (Ed.). (2002). *Creating campus community: In search of Ernest Boyer's legacy.* San Francisco: Jossey-Bass.

Nussbaum, M. (2003). Compassion & terror. *Daedalus, 132*(1), 10–26.

Page, O. C. (2003, Winter). Promoting diversity in academic leadership. *New Directions for Higher Education, 124*, 79–86.

Walshok, M. (1999). Strategies for building the infrastructure that supports the engaged campus. In R. Bringle, R. Games, & E. Malloy (Eds.), *Colleges and universities as citizens* (pp. 74–96). Boston: Allyn & Bacon.

2

SHIFTING THE ORGANIZATIONAL PERSPECTIVE ON DIVERSITY

Institutional and Academic Change

Kenneth Bruffee (2002), in a provocative article in the higher educational periodical, *Change*, offers both a conceptual and practical approach to linking institutional change to diversity and civic responsibility. He uses the concept of "cultural boundaries" as a structural analogy and realistic locus of change. For decades colleges and universities have accepted the boundaries and power differentials that define the organizational placing of traditional groups (student, faculty, administrators, researchers, staff) and culture-specific groups, that is, those that possess culture-specific identities.

Bruffee contends that current institutional structures sustain a gratifying measure of tolerance, but do not allow for the development of common ground. He stresses that "taking the common ground requires learning the intricacies and tack of renegotiating membership in one's own culture and of finding new occasions to negotiate across the boundaries that divide cultural communities" (p. 15). Multicultural liberal education has attempted since the 1970s to permeate traditional ways of teaching and the curriculum with varied success, and each subsequent decade has presented a new set of political realties. Leaders and multidimensional thinkers in the academy should identify new ways to engage different groups in creating a revised framework that eliminates stratification, concrete borders, glass ceilings, and other political, social, and targeted impediments that pass as normal institutional structures and processes. Such engagement should encourage a sense of ownership among those who are asked to consider institutional alterations, especially when doing so adds some risk as these individuals pursue their traditional responsibilities.

Campus leaders must accept that crossing boundaries can result in an intimidating and precarious landscape as naïve students, traditional faculty, risk-averse leaders, new immigrants, American ethic minorities, and international students become aware of the implications of solidarity and the distressing details of attaining it. Finding common ground is not a passive act. It involves seeing around corners and anticipating consequences—characteristics that can generally be associated with effective leadership, but they are necessities for those who seek to cross boundaries.

Finding common ground begins with an analysis of institutional values and operational principles, in other words, an introspective self-study. An attempt by campus leaders to place an overlay of diversity-related activities or structures on top of unexamined principles will only produce transient and ineffective outcomes. Research institutions, for example, are predisposed to passionately support those values and principles that underscore their identity in the national research community. As such, the institutional incorporation of diversity and globalism at such institutions must account for this reality. Two-year institutions with an open-door admissions process attract diverse populations in increasing numbers, yet many fail to use such diversity as an asset, and no one suffers as a result more than students.

Leadership is the force that drives a cultural shift on campus in less challenging and more accepted areas such as enhancements in technology. However, to sustain a cultural shift that supports diversity is a much more daunting task, one that requires acumen, courage, and integrity. In most cases the community may be asked to revisit the core identity of the institution, not so much to replace it but to realize the implicit potential it contains and to renew a commitment to sustain and enhance that identity.

Core Principles and Organizational Change

Some institutions seek to root transformative change for diversity within a core set of principles that becomes both the guiding ethos and a pragmatic blueprint for organizational change. These statements tend to be more complete and inclusive than the institution's mission statement, and are often included as a legitimate component of formal campus diversity plans or of less formal initiatives. Campus conversations about diversity become more robust when that language parallels the vernacular used in strategic planning, committee work, trustee considerations, faculty development programs, etc.

As institutions embrace diversity, core principles can serve one or more functions, including as a

- Compass (Where in the organization should we target our diversity efforts?)
- Barometer (How committed are we to and passionate about diversity and organizational change?)
- Billboard (Hey, you, these are our core beliefs about diversity!)
- Raison d'être (Unidiversity—I am inclusive, therefore I am!)
- Warning sign (Transgressors will not be tolerated!)
- Beacon (The institution's affirmation of the relationship between diversity and excellence!)
- Binding force (An institutional culture that promotes active inclusion!)

At many institutions, even the most well-intentioned core principles regarding diversity do not evolve far beyond grandiose platitudes. Sometimes there is tacit delusion that diversity is affecting organizational progress and change, and such a delusion is easier to sustain when the institutional leadership provides little direction and when there is little, if any, critical discourse about diversity. One strong indicator of such a situation can be found in the absence of accountability to promote basic areas of excellence such as teaching and learning outcomes.

A smaller fraternity of colleges and universities translates diversity principles into the conceptual models that precede organizational implementation and change. At the most fundamental level, such institutions appear to "walk the talk" about diversity. A more intricate examination reveals concrete indicators that can serve as evidence that institutions are committed to core beliefs about diversity. More specifically, how did these institutions initiate organizational transformation? What actions or processes facilitated structural change? What differentiates a commitment to core principles as opposed to diversity activities? Why are institutional leaders hesitant to create the conditions for the open discourse that must precede a serious commit-ment to change? Throughout this book I contend that the organizational change associated with diversity enhances attempts to support excellence in other important areas as well. Academic bureaucrats can be capable adminis-trators and financial managers, and they can produce organizational change, but they are seldom characterized as transformational leaders or leaders of cultural change. Twenty-first-century campuses benefit from the vision of this latter group.

From Vision to Core Identity: A Diversity Plan

Translating a campus vision of diversity into some segment of the core iden-tity most likely will be facilitated by an incremental planning process. The rate of change can be regulated by the degree to which traditional processes that have historically guided and shaped the institution can be used, rather than by the need to develop a new process and have it accepted. Many cam-puses that have committed to change have selected development of a formal diversity plan as the primary vehicle that not only moves between a past and future vision, but also provides a working blueprint for the critical dialogue that will result.

While there is no consensus across institutional types concerning an agreed-upon format for a campus diversity plan, those colleges and universi-ties that appear to move diversity from just a vision to actual aspects of the core identity exhibit common strengths. Among these are the following (An-derson, 1996):

- The diversity plan makes a statement about where an institution wants to go and what it wants to become in the 21st century. By doing so, it represents a public declaration of what it values and perceives as worth pursuing.
- The diversity plan involves broad and collaborative inclusion across many sectors and constituencies (faculty, staff, students, administra-tors, and community groups).
- The diversity plan incorporates clear evidence of institutional support, senior-level leadership and accountability, and a willingness to grapple with a range of issues, including some that may arouse political and emotional sensitivities.

- A planning process was used that affected significant layers of institutional functioning and offered some groups a sense of ownership.
- The priorities associated with the diversity plan parallel other major university initiatives such as retention and graduation concerns, development of a receptive and inclusive campus community, attainment of general education competencies, etc.
- The plan does not violate the valued principles of shared responsibility and shared governance.
- The diversity plan specifies what criteria will be used as part of both formative and summative assessment.
- The diversity plan receives early review by and input from critical faculty groups.
- The diversity plan addresses, in functional ways, curricular and pedagogical transformation and the expected outcomes associated with each. (p. 2)

One of the major assumptions of an effective diversity plan is that, if we increase the number of diverse faculty and staff, then other aspects of campus diversity will improve as well. This shifts part of the institutional burden onto diverse groups that are not usually empowered to produce institutional change along critical dimensions. An effective diversity plan does not offer grandiose or unrealistic performance expectations for diverse faculty, administration, and staff. Moreover, regular monitoring and mentoring of diverse faculty by senior faculty can benefit the department, college, and university.

Can Diversity Plans Influence Discourse?

Diversity plans serve various purposes for the colleges and universities that develop and implement them. Some plans are structured as strategic action plans that include timetables and sources of accountability, others are less focused, yet they also send a message about the institution's commitment to equity and an inclusive climate. Recognizing that competing campus politics surround instituting a diversity plan, it is important that we understand how such policy documents frame perceptions about diversity and the discourses that accompany the plan's evolution.

Susan Iverson (2005, 2006), a faculty member at Kent State University, systematically examined 21 diversity action plans at land-grant research universities over a five-year period. Using the method of policy discourse analysis that included an iterative process of coding, she sought to identify images of diversity, and the problems and solutions related to diversity as represented in diversity action plans. She focuses on four fundamental questions:

- What discourses are used?
- How are problems represented?
- How are solutions represented?
- What are predominant images?

The analysis yields 10 types of discourse, and as a result of the images produced as part of the discourse, a standard emerges to assess groups in terms of their progress and success. The discourse types and four questions serve as the column and row headings in a revealing matrix that can be generalized to other campuses and organizations with similar plans. The entire matrix can be viewed in Appendix A.

Findings indicate that dominant discourses of access and disadvantage coalesce to produce images of diverse persons as outsiders to the institution, at risk before and after entering the university and dependent on it for higher education success. Further, discourses of marketplace, excellence, and managerialism contribute to shaping the impersonal images of diverse individuals as a commodity, and a discourse of democracy emerges as an alternative, constructing the diverse individual in a more personal image as a change agent. It is important to note that the types of prevailing discourse that shape group images construct and maintain the varied perceptions of diverse groups.

Leadership and Change

While it is often assumed that top-down leadership initiates and sustains institutional transformation, in the case of diversity and organizational change, it is rare that a significant cadre of committed leaders would be at the same institution at the same time to effect change across boundaries, structures, and divisions. Senior leadership is vital; in fact, it is indispensable to any serious attempt to integrate diversity and/or globalism into the academy. Yet, the dynamism that can fuel such inclusion slowly or, in rare cases, by quantum leaps, comes from those at other levels of the organization who recognize and seek organizational change and who can better assess the pulse of a campus. Such individuals do so not in an oppositional way, but for positive reasons: excellence, success, altruism, equity, ethics, loyalty (to students, colleagues, and the institution), and other intrinsic drivers. This group also thrives within a climate that expects accountability and rewards commitment to change.

In her book on organizational change in the 21st century, Meyerson (2001) refers to "tempered radical[s]" as those who operate as change agents at varied levels within the organization. They bring their ideas, ideals, agendas, vision, emotions, knowledge, and identities to the cultural systems on a campus. In the case of diversity, they work from within to challenge traditions that are not inclusive, and to restructure the organization's capacity to change. They may be student leaders, program managers, assistant deans, members of the staff and/or faculty senate, etc. They may use their existing campus organizations or create new ones, and they often suspend their personal and political partisanship as they pursue a more challenging goal. The history of organizational change at colleges and universities is permeated by the passion and actions of those who, similar to tempered radicals, conjoin their actions and energies with that of institutional leaders.

Goldberg and Greenberg (2004) suggest that multilevel change agents become successful when they learn to analyze an organization's cultural system and then determine how best to introduce a change initiative such as diversity. In some cases this might involve linking powerful ideals (multicultural liberal learning and academic freedom), structures (global curriculum and a core or general education curriculum), or processes (diversity recruitment and retention of faculty and the traditional criteria associated with promotion and tenure). Those who are involved in the change process develop a sense of empowerment and legitimacy as they slowly introduce change while not threatening what is most valued and most powerful in the system.

Challenging Organizational Myopia

At many colleges and universities, leaders not only bemoan the homogeneity of student and faculty racial and ethnic backgrounds, but also assume a causal link between this lack of representational and structural diversity and the institution's ability to promote meaningful educational outcomes. In other words, "If we ain't got diversity then we can't produce diversity experiences." Such a contention, however, can deenergize a campus and prevent it from promoting those practices and outcomes that reflect educational excellence and the diversity mission. While it is important for institutions to pursue demographic diversity among students, staff, and faculty, this cannot be used as an excuse to avoid more fundamental considerations about diversity.

Academic leaders should refrain from making broad generalizations about diversity and their campus when such statements represent opinions, conjecture, and unsubstantiated conclusions. Instead, they should capitalize on their local expertise to formulate and answer questions about the nature and impact of the diversity experience, especially among faculty and students. Kuh and Umbach (2005) summarize the findings of two complementary national projects whose results shed significant light on what we can conclude about diversity experiences at liberal arts colleges. One project, the National Survey on Student Engagement (NSSE), represents a comprehensive annual survey of first-year and senior students. The sample that was drawn from liberal arts colleges involved 17,640 enrolled students. The second project, Documenting Effective Educational Practices (DEEP), involved 20 colleges and universities that exhibited higher-than-predicted graduation rates and NSSE scores and that committed to fundamental organizational change in many critical areas.

In terms of how varied institutions compare with each other, the NSSE data offer several conclusions:

- There appears to be a higher frequency of diversity experiences for students at liberal arts colleges than there is at other types of institutions.
- Despite their shortcomings in actual diversity (representation), liberal arts colleges appear to have diversity-rich learning environments.
- Diversity experiences are positively associated with other important outcomes (problem solving, critical thinking, active and collaborative learning, a supportive campus, and personal growth and understanding).
- The climate for diversity is positively related to almost all of the engagement and gains measures.

In terms of actual practice, the DEEP data also offer important conclusions:

- A visible commitment to diversity was common among all institutions involved in the project.
- Liberal arts colleges exhibited a willingness to implement programs and practices that encourage and support cross-racial and cross-cultural interactions.
- Diverse perspectives in the classroom and the curriculum are essential. They are complemented by policies and practices that heighten student exposure.

These data are important because they challenge the beliefs and arguments of those leaders who allow organizational constriction because of limitations in representational and structural diversity. Such a scenario says as much about institutional will and leadership as it does about the impact of diversity engagement and experiences. Even with limited resources, DEEP institutions have aligned the strategies and processes that are necessary for fundamental change.

Committed Traditionalists and Tempered Radicals: A Partnership for Institution Transformation and Diversity

On most campuses the political and academic discourse about such concepts as diversity, multiculturalism, and globalism is often complex and ambiguous. Despite our best efforts, this campus discourse is shaped, and sometimes corrupted, by external pressures. One of the more difficult tasks associated with formal institutionalization of diversity involves setting the balance between what is traditional and most valued, and how requests for change are perceived as affecting institutional image and reputation, faculty concerns and vitality, campus politics, changing demographics, and organizational structural integrity.

Campus leaders must combine their historical memory with their current knowledge of the critical junctures where change has the best opportunity for successful implementation and impact. The loci for change, together with expected timelines, will vary across internal areas. The following example offers a glimpse of how such change occurred within an entire college.

Babson College is a private and nationally ranked business college located in Wellesley, Massachusetts. Since 1982, it has developed a model of Executive

Education that emphasizes a cycle of continuous learning, interdisciplinary integration, intellectual diversity, real-world experiences, thoughtful leadership, and social ethics. Babson offers programs that provide leaders with the perspective and solutions that are necessary for the 21st century. For example, it is one of the few business schools that offer a unique executive development program for women who are determined to succeed at the next level. A key partner in delivering this program is Babson's Center for Women's Leadership.

It is the structure of Babson's undergraduate curriculum and experience that differentiates it from its peers, and also serves as a case study for organizational transformation and diversity. The curriculum is three-tiered (foundation, intermediate, and advanced), and students take courses across the curriculum in both management and liberal arts. The curriculum is also based on competencies or learning outcomes that ask students to analyze the disciplines within the context of a world composed of diverse cultures, ways of knowing, and situational contexts. Goldberg and Greenberg (2004) provide an excellent summary of the impact of the Babson approach to teaching and learning on its graduates. They report that students:

- learn to apply a cultural lens to their fundamental biases and perceptions about business and management;
- reframe their views by recognizing the impact that culture, structure, and politics have on individual and organizational success;
- understand the cultural foundations of the collection and use of quantitative data; and
- experience conversations across the disciplinary boundaries of liberal arts and management courses (p. 20).

The faculty at Babson use modes of pedagogical and scholarly inquiry that immerse the student into the discipline, while also broadening his or her consciousness of social justice, social entrepreneurship, and recognition of the need for social change.

The organizational transformation of Babson has evolved over two decades without shattering the faculty's fundamental belief in academic freedom and excellence. Diversity and globalism permeate the institutional culture, and the finished product is a student who embodies the purpose of the Babson Student Core Competencies.

This progression to excellence would generate upheaval and a crisis of leadership at many comparable business schools, which would fear the charge a political partisanship (aka "leaning to the left"). Babson exhibits the courage to place oppositional discourse in an analytic framework that asks students and faculty to examine cultural systems through an intellectual lens that may reveal liberal, conservative, and/or apolitical power dynamics. The courage to question underscores their courage to change.

Strategic Directions: Dos and Don'ts

There is an impressive body of literature on many topical areas associated with leadership and organizational change in both the public and academic arenas. There currently exist well-developed models of leadership and blueprints for change concerning diversity and globalism in the public and corporate sectors, more so than in the academy. Virtually all Fortune 500 companies, global corporations, the armed forces, city and state governments, and the health care industry can provide evidence of measurable goals and objectives that support a concrete commitment to diversity and to leadership that underscores such commitment.

As an example, the National Academy of Sciences Institute of Medicine issued an important report (Smedley, Butler, & Bristow, 2004), which included recommendations that are not only relevant to institutions of higher education but are transformative in nature as well. The thematic nature of the report is one of urgency and fundamental (institutional) change. The recommendations include:

- Reconceptualizing admissions policies and practices
- Reducing financial barriers to underrepresented minorities in health professions education
- Using accreditation as a key to increase diversity in health professions
- Transforming the institutional climate to enhance diversity
- Developing additional research and data collection on diversity and its benefits (p. 14)

The report's authors represent a distinguished committee whose members were chosen for their special competencies in diversity and the health professions. On its surface the report represents an external voice affiliated with the network of health care training programs. In reality it is a planning document that is applicable across program types and one that can support leadership decisions for change at colleges and universities, especially those with health-related disciplines, nursing, and medicine.

The irony of this state of affairs is that colleges and universities purport to represent an arena of academic freedom where the critical discourse about contemporary topics and challenges associated with academic discussions about diversity and globalism can be discussed free of criticism and intimidation. The academy also purports to be the melting pot of intellectual insights and new definitions of organizational excellence, the locus of finding common ground, and the existential and practical context where leadership can be tested and exercised for the common good. Perhaps the fundamental issue is that applying public reports that address diversity as a compelling interest questions some academic programs and departments' commitment to excellence.

Among the many explanations for this visible dichotomy and/or the degree of separation is the fact that the public and corporate sectors have identified an evolutionary synchrony among diversity, organizational processes, and the most important organizational outcomes. Within the academy the tendency to overintellectualize, overpoliticize, decentralize, and homogenize the diversity discussion precludes attaching it to other core issues and processes. Moreover, campus leaders' vision (but not always their commitment) can be skewed toward that camouflage of change but not toward its substantive grounding. After all, challenging program effectiveness or faculty competency and/or commitment may be a recipe for controversy for any leader, but more so for those who lack the courage to question.

I offer eight mandatory considerations that campus leaders need to ponder if they intend to stay true to their commitment to diversity/globalism and institutional change.

1. Avoid abstract language or ambiguous meaning about both institutional change and diversity. As leaders shape their conceptual and semantic statements, they must account for three factors: the public nature of their statements, the constituents who represent the target audience(s), and the linguistic cogency that will or will not capture attention and make an impression. While associates may prepare written drafts or suggest ideas to leaders, the ultimate responsibililty for clarity and consistency and the external visualization of the message rests solely with the leader.

2. Translation of core principles should be grounded in the historical patterns of organizational change that can be perceived as having a relationship to the proposed incorporation of diversity. Campus leaders must identify those existing traditional structures and imperatives that can drag new ones with them. For example, can the current general education or core curriculum drive the diversification of a transformed curriculum? Can the historical policies, practices, and regulations in human resources absorb the equitable demands of an increasingly diverse workforce?

3. Cultivate that aspect of your leadership style that alternates between seeing the big picture and recognizing the junctures of less obvious but equally important incremental change. A simple axiom will do here: there will be few opportunities for macro change (so capitalize when they occur) and many instances where incremental innovation represents the next logical and necessary step. While this is true in terms of institutional functioning in general, attentiveness to a macro versus micro analysis of diversity may represent new territory for some leaders.

4. Leaders should analyze in depth several institutions where at least moderate change has occurred, is visible, and is making a difference in diversity and institutional change. For example, most campus leaders are familiar with the public summaries of the historic Supreme Court ruling (June 2003) that upheld the University of Michigan's contention that diversity in the classroom translates to beneficial and wide-ranging social values. However, they are much less aware, and in come cases ignorant, of the historical context, factual background, and social/psychological implications that provided the evidentiary basis for this case. Decades of preparation are what bound diversity to institutional change and ultimately vindicated their position.

5. To what degree are institutional leaders' decisions about diversity guided by the wisdom and expertise of multidimensional and analytical thinkers? This core team of advisers may not reflect what is visualized in the organizational chart because the chart may exist for reasons more germane to traditional organizational functioning. A valuable exercise would be to take the existing organizational chart, expunge current names and titles, and replace them with those who

represent the most effective analytical, multidimensional, and practical thinkers about diversity and organizational change.

6. As a leader you must plan your response to external pressures and outside forces when they agree or disagree with your decisions about diversity and change. Those who initiate external pressure often expect one of two extremes: major institutional reform or complete adherence to existing stability. Thus, as a leader you must master the techniques that allow you to balance external expectations and your commitment to a fundamental decision-making process.

7. When leaders react to a point of progression where implementation of diversity reforms is the next logical step, do not decentralize before reaching a broad consensus. Interorganizational agreement about the implementation of diversity reforms facilitates the speed and effectiveness of such reforms. The alliance between student affairs and academic affairs, for example, is an absolute necessity when considering diversity reform. Thus, agreements must be struck, a priori, that benefit both sides and preclude any potential objections.

8. Special attention must be paid to the roles and responsibilities of the chief academic officer in any discussion about diversity and organizational change. The most significant and lasting gains will occur when diversity is linked in concrete ways to the institution's teaching, learning, and research mission. Thus, any formal evaluation of that office must involve "real" organizational contributions to diversity reforms. Provosts and vice presidents of academic affairs need a special level of leadership to contend with the traditional beliefs and biases of faculty, academic administrators, and students.

Academic Mission Scorecard

The primacy of the academic mission is perhaps the most important vehicle involved in the development of inclusive excellence, a term that blends diversity, inclusion, standards of academic excellence, and institutional renewal. Its significance cannot be understated or overshadowed. While other administrators may have indirect responsibilities involving some aspect of inclusive excellence, several offices should be evaluated in terms of responsibility and accountability. They are as follows:

- office of the provost and/or vice president for academic affairs (vice provost and/or associate provost)
- academic deans and their respective associate academic deans (undergraduate and graduate)
- vice provost (associate provost) for undergraduate studies/affairs/programs
- vice president for instruction
- department chairs or heads
- senior administrative officers for diversity, enrollment management, and/or assessment/institutional research

In other chapters I have attempted to outline institutional limitations that preclude implementation of a diversity vision and plan, so I will not belabor that point here. Instead, it is more useful when markers exist that chief executive officers (CEOs), chief academic officers (CAOs), and the external community can designate as points of progress; targets of opportunity; intersections with broader university values, goals, and objectives; and indicators of leadership and accountability. Considering the importance of diversity and globalism to the future of colleges and universities in the 21st century, the question of whether an academic scorecard should exist is a moot point. Such an evaluative and diagnostic tool should be valid, reliable, timely, equitable, purposeful, and offer feedback that leads to continuous improvement.

While an academic scorecard can reflect individual institutions' unique characteristics and idiosyncrasies, a more common template adds value as an interinstitutional yardstick of comparison. Thus, the following characteristics are useful as a first stage of institutional reflection.

1. The chief academic officer should disseminate a public document that defines and communicates the value of linking diversity and globalism to academics, to academic excellence, and to the mission of his or her office. The CAO should monitor the development and quality of similar efforts at the college and department level.
2. The diversity/globalism academic document should chronicle the initiatives, programs, courses, services, etc., that demonstrate the university's success in creating and sustaining a diverse intellectual and social community. Moreover, the relationship between this document

and other important academic documents should be explained and validated.

3. The CAO's administrative/academic team should function proactively, as one of the major leadership teams that campus constituencies associate with diversity. While team members should react to situations, it is more important for them to be proactive, to use foresight, planning, and courageous leadership to solve problems and deal with issues. Valuable members of the team should never be offered as sacrificial lambs when controversy arises.

4. The CAO should conduct a substantive evaluation of academic administrators that is neither arbitrary nor subjective but that includes specific criteria on diversity efforts and achievements. Where appropriate, this evaluation should represent a substantive aspect of the administrator's overall assessment.

5. The CAO, dean, and academic department chairs/heads should articulate how a commitment to success and excellence is reflected across the various segments of diversity (racial diversity, gender and gender orientation diversity, cultural diversity, religious diversity, ideological diversity, diverse abilities, political diversity, class diversity, geographical diversity, organizational and/or workforce diversity, etc.). It is assumed that the emphasis in many cases will be discipline-, program-, institution-, and constituent-specific.

6. Classroom instructors should be engaged in critical conversations about pedagogy, diversity, globalism, and inclusion in the classroom. These conversations can be outcomes-, discipline-, and/or research-based. The role of the CAO and other administrators is to identify what motivates faculty to take ownership of such conversations. Examples include departmental curriculum development grants, allocations to the operating budgets of departments that excel in diversity efforts, significant involvement of the Faculty Teaching Center to provide training, evidence of a certification process to guide the development of a diverse pool of prospective candidates, and an assessment plan that provides continuous feedback on the impact of teaching, learning, and inclusion.

7. The CAO should convene a series of provost/VP academic affairs–sponsored forums on diversity and globalism that emphasize very

specific topical outcomes, such as Expanding the Evidentiary Basis for Diversity and Academic Excellence; Scrutinizing the Academic Policies and Structures That Enhance Diversity; Diversity and Successful Learning Communities; and Diversity as a Research Agenda.

8. The CAO should closely monitor the campus climate as it affects underrepresented groups. This involves shared interactions and the freedom to speak openly and truthfully. Once or twice a semester, the CAO and deans should host a breakfast or luncheon meeting with one underrepresented group or engage in structured surveys or focus groups. Such gatherings are especially important to underrepresented faculty and graduate students on predominantly White campuses.

These considerations can be condensed into an evaluation tool that can assess campus perceptions of academic leadership and competency relative to diversity issues and outcomes. One example of a survey instrument that could be used for this purpose appears in Appendix B. The 11-item questionnaire uses statements that are behavioral indicators and asks respondents to rate them on a five-point Likert scale as evidence of leadership and competency. The evaluation of actual behaviors is a better indicator of transformational leadership than a campus community's abstract perception of leadership potential. The following are two examples of the questions:

Closely monitors the campus climate as it is experienced by underrepresented groups.

Leadership   _____ _____ _____ _____ _____
              Exhibits No   Exhibits   Exhibits
              Evidence   Moderate   Significant
                                        Evidence   Evidence

Competency   _____ _____ _____ _____ _____
              Exhibits No   Exhibits   Exhibits
              Evidence   Moderate   Significant
                                        Evidence   Evidence

Raises the level of sophistication about the critical discourse on diversity and globalism associated with their area of responsibility.

Leadership   _____ _____ _____ _____ _____
              Exhibits No   Exhibits   Exhibits
              Evidence   Moderate   Significant
                                        Evidence   Evidence

Competency					
Exhibits No Evidence		Exhibits Moderate Evidence		Exhibits Significant Evidence	

The results of this type of survey can be used in a variety of ways, none of which should be punitive. For example, a CEO or CAO could develop a snapshot of where the strengths and weaknesses associated with leadership and diversity are located in an organizational chart. Campus leaders could incorporate the survey results as one of several sources of self-assessment feedback. An institution could establish cohort comparisons such as department chairs across colleges, academic versus administrative leaders, gender comparisons, etc. While open-ended survey questions ("provide examples of this person's leadership qualities") place no restrictions on respondents' perceptions, they also do not target the qualities deemed to be most important for a leadership role that supports diversity.

A Systematic Analysis of Institutional Readiness

When colleges and universities prepare for their regional accreditation site visits they use a self-study as the framework for a holistic and balanced diagnosis of the institution. In fact, this introspective analysis may represent that moment when leaders do contemplate significant change. Can institutional leaders use a comparable analysis to assess both the current state of affairs and the future readiness of a campus to embrace significant change associated with diversity?

The answer is a resolute yes! Campuses that have moved toward the cutting edge in their thinking about diversity and institutional change have used analytic and collaborative processes that have generated systematic frameworks for change. Such frameworks are underscored by a willingness to ask the difficult questions, to generate and use data effectively, to select effective strategies, and to maintain accountability as a significant goal.

The challenges of becoming a learning-centered institution are magnified when an institution commits to integrating diversity and globalism in a meaningful way across the institution and, especially, within a teaching-learning paradigm. In some cases the conditions for change favor an institution thus mollifying the stressors that often accompany transformational change. Perhaps a larger number of institutions struggle to identify an appropriate point to begin to marshal their respective energies toward a learning-centered identity. One potential solution would be to review existing institutional data through a more analytical lens and identify critical junctures that would allow a more systematic and successful application of strategies. Such an approach also presents the opportunity to generate one or more baselines of institutional data that benefit both the framing of "snapshots" and the development of a longitudinal picture. For example, examining grades by type of course can reveal the 10 academic courses that yield the highest percentage of student failure and course withdrawals, which should suggest problems with teaching effectiveness and student learning (or a lack of learning-centeredness). Further analysis may reveal differential grade performance by race and preparation level, with students of color often exhibiting the lowest performance. While such data are available to institutions at any time, such analysis only becomes a triggering mechanism for action among that small percentage of institutions that genuinely support both diversity and a learning-centered identity. Some faculty who experience difficulty in academic courses with diverse students identify the student as the primary source of failure, in essence, blaming the victim While this may be true for a specific category of students, it generally does not apply across a range of learners and over a long period.

In a learning-centered environment, systematic analysis of data and processes targets the real source of student problems: Is the student underprepared, or unmotivated, or simply using an inappropriate learning strategy? Is the instructor providing effective feedback when student errors occur? Does the instructor facilitate other cognitive skills as he or she covers the content of the course? Are there difficulties with the curriculum such that it interferes with student learning? Are transitional factors affecting semester-to-semester retention? Occasionally, campus teams work together to gather and interpret data related to these questions and to develop success models for students of color. The Diversity Scorecard Project, developed by Estela Mara Bensimon (2004) at the Center for Urban Education at the University of Southern California, gathers data related to four dimensions associated with performance, diversity, and equity: access, retention, institutional receptivity, and excellence. The project encourages participating institutions to use a systematic, evidence-based approach to examine critical factors.

Perhaps more than any other state system, I have acknowledged publicly my admiration for the significant efforts in the state of Washington that have altered the educational landscape there in terms of assessing, planning, and implementing projects to improve the academic success and engagement of students of color. I served as an external reviewer for several years to one project funded by the Ford Foundation, thus I was able to observe part of the evolution of the framework. Before 1996–97 many of the two- and four-year institutions had attempted to address diversity in purposeful ways within their own institutions. But in June 1998, a group of 43 faculty, administrators, and staff members gathered to address a primary question and to develop a framework for diversity assessment and planning—this collaborative design would serve as the catalyst for institutional change. The simple question was, "What can the community/technical college system do to help students of color achieve more academic success?"

Lardner and Coats (2004) outlined the final general recommendations that emerged from this work:

1. Retention: address the issue by developing a plan based on careful listening to student voices.
2. Professional development: offer staff/faculty training workshops on specific topics on a regional basis.
3. Link diversity to accreditation: work with the accreditation liaisons.
4. Clarify system goals related to diversity for use by individuals and by institutions.
5. Washington State Board staffs convene groups to share ideas and training.

Following presentation of these recommendations, the Critical Moments project evolved, and seven retreats were held around the state. The central command post for these efforts was the Washington Center for Improving the Quality of Undergraduate Education at Evergreen State University. It was during these discussions that the idea of linking diversity efforts to accountability and accreditation was born, and it became the cornerstone of the framework.

According to Lardner and Coats (2004, p. 7), the purpose of the framework is "to provide campuses with a tool they can use to assess their efforts in promoting and supporting the academic achievement of students of color." The framework encouraged institutions to engage in internal and external data gathering and to use methods that provided the most significant yield. It uses a matrix that addresses eight major categories, each of which has multiple subcategories. Each category is scrutinized to determine the following:

- Purpose (what you want to know; questions or issues to consider with respect to the subcategory)
- Scope (type/source of data)
- Measures (where we would get the data)
- Results (what are your findings; what do the data say?)
- Recommendations for action

The beauty of this planning document is its utilitarian value: it can be adopted and/or modified across institutional type. Its systematic nature allows easy insertion into accreditation reviews, strategic plans, college plans, etc. The iteration of such a wonderful framework, with its system-level implications, offers hope and encouragement to those institutions that continue to struggle with diversity and its promise (or threat) for institutional change.

The Courage to Question

The feedback loop concerning this discussion always returns to leadership and transformational change and the expectation that leaders must guide the discourse associated with intentional questions. It is important that institutions begin with a series of questions with which they can feel confident (Bresciani, Zelna, & Anderson, 2004). The following two categories offer examples:

Leadership: Describe how leaders provide effective leadership in fostering diversity and success within the organization, taking into account the needs and expectations of all key stakeholders

- How does the leadership team communicate and clearly incorporate the values of diversity and student, faculty, and staff success in the organization's directions and expectations?
- How does the leadership team communicate expectations about diversity and accountability throughout the organization?
- How does the leadership team seek future opportunities to incorporate and embed the values of diversity and success in the organization?

- How does the leadership team maintain a climate conducive to learning, equity, and success for students, staff, and faculty?
- How does the leadership team incorporate the views and efforts of all constituencies (underrepresented and majority) into the leadership system?

Organizational Strategy: Describe how the organization determines the requirements and expectations of students, staff, faculty, and other important constituents relative to satisfaction, support, and the success of diversity efforts.

- How are implementation responsibilities decided and assigned?
- How does the organization track organizational performance relative to diversity plans/goals?
- How are process barriers (that impede progress) identified and incorporated into the strategic plans and actions?

Other categories include Selection and Use of Data and Information; Education, Training, and Development; Education and Support Process; and Results. The questions were developed using the framework of the criteria associated with the Baldrige Award for total quality, a national award for organizational excellence. The complete listing is in Appendix C.

Despite their assertions that they and their institutions welcome the change that accompanies their emergence as a 21st-century institution of educational excellence, campus leaders must offer evidence of a bold vision and systematic way of planning that energizes the campus community to engage in the long-term efforts that actually allow diversity and institutional change to complement one another.

References

Anderson, J. A. (1996). *An external review of the five-year diversity plan and evaluation for Colorado State University*. Unpublished paper.

Bennett, J. M., & Bennett, M. J. (2004). Developing intercultural sensitivity: An integrative approach to global and domestic diversity. In D. Landis, J. M. Bennett, & M. J. Bennett (Eds.), *Handbook of intercultural training*. (3rd ed., pp. 147–165). Thousand Oaks, CA: Sage.

Bensimon, E. M. (2004). The diversity scorecard: A learning approach to institutional change. *Change, 36*(1), 45–52.

Bresciani, M. J., Zelna, C. L., & Anderson, J. (2004). *Assessing student learning and development.* Washington, DC: National Association of Student Personnel Administrators.

Bruffee, K. (2002). Taking the common ground: Beyond cultural identity. *Change, 34*(1), 10–17.

Gambrill, E. (2005). *Critical thinking in clinical practice: Improving the accuracy of judgments and decisions about clients* (2nd ed.). New York: Wiley.

Goldberg, E. S., & Greenburg, D. (2004). What's a cultural studies curriculum doing in a college like this? *Liberal Education, 90*(3), 16–25.

Iverson, S. (2005). *A policy discourse analysis of U.S. land-grant university diversity action plans.* Unpublished doctoral dissertation, University of Maine, Orono

Iverson, S. (2006, summer). *Diversity initiatives: Toward a multicultural campus.* Paper presented at meeting of the Commission on Human Resources and Social Change, Washington, DC.

Kuh, G. D., & Umbach, P. D. (2005). Experiencing diversity: What can we learn from liberal arts colleges? *Liberal Education, 91*(1), 14–21.

Lardner, E., & Coats, R. (2004). *A collaboratively designed catalyst for change. Introducing the framework for diversity assessment and planning.* Olympia, WA: Center for Improving the Quality of Undergraduate Education.

Meyerson, D. (2001). *Tempered radicals: How people use difference to inspire change.* Boston, MA: Harvard Business School Press.

Smedley, B. D., Butler, A. S., & Bristow, L. R. (2004). *In the nation's compelling interest: Ensuring diversity in the healthcare workforce. A report by the National Academy of Sciences Institute of Medicine.* Washington, DC: National Academy Press.

3

SHAPING THE ACADEMIC
DISCUSSION ABOUT
DIVERSITY

On many campuses the academic discussion about diversity, especially one that involves the faculty, does not always conform to
the parameters of other discussions that reflect what these faculty
value. Among the reasons why this is the case, two stand out:

- diversity is not associated with the extrinsic and intrinsic incentives
  that motivate faculty, and
- diversity is not a part of the regular business of academic departments.

For faculty to value diversity, it must be connected to traditional extrinsic incentives such as promotion and tenure, reduced teaching loads, faculty
stipends and salary bonuses, and faculty development initiatives. Another
important extrinsic incentive is identification of new research topics associated with diversity and the increase in research productivity (publications,
grants, etc.) that would result. Intrinsic incentives are more complex to identify and execute, and they tend to be associated with:

- higher-order needs of faculty such as competency and service;
- personal satisfaction and attainment; and
- shared goals among faculty colleagues or shared outcomes such as establishing a learning community or enhancing the quality of the graduate student experience.

Assumptions about which incentives motivate faculty more than others
should be grounded in actual feedback that reflects faculty's perceptions.

Since faculty communities differ across institutional types and across departments within the same institution, uniform responses are unlikely. The criteria associated with effective assessment of faculty perceptions, beliefs, and attitudes on diversity suggest using such authentic assessments as surveys, focus groups, or other qualitative measures of reflective feedback.

Figure 3.1 offers one way to determine faculty opinions about the potential incentives they associate with diversity and diversity-related issues. Faculty are asked to rank order the list of 13 potential incentives in the first column, in terms of their personal rankings, by placing a number in the second column. The incentive that is most important/valuable is ranked as 1, while the one that is least important/valuable is ranked as 13.

In the third column individual faculty are asked to comment on their perceptions of their colleagues. How do they think their colleagues would

FIGURE 3.1
Faculty Incentives and Diversity

Incentive Associated With Diversity	*Personal Rankings*	*Perceptions of Your Faculty Colleagues*
1. Tenure		
2. Promotion		
3. Salary bonus/stipend		
4. Reduced teaching load		
5. Faculty development funds		
6. Travel funds		
7. Enhanced instructional skills		
8. Enhanced sense of inter-personal competence		
9. Facilitating a sense of community at the institution		
10. Identification of new research topics		
11. Increased interactions with students who are diverse		
12. Facilitating competencies among diverse populations		
13. Enhanced ability to recruit diverse undergraduate and graduate students		

rank order the same list of incentives? Are there noticeable or exaggerated differences between the two columns; if so, why might they exist?

Where should we expect the lower rankings to occur in either column? Historically, faculty's sacred cow has been ownership of the criteria associated with tenure and promotion. Although administrative input has been part of P&T (input from deans and department chairs) decisions to varying degrees, diversity has not enjoyed this privilege. This state of affairs is even more exaggerated at research universities, where publications and research funding are the primary criteria. Administrators must exhibit careful judgment when they choose to nudge faculty toward considering diversity in the faculty review process, especially as it pertains to academic freedom and governance.

Where should we expect larger differences between the two columns, which would indicate a discrepancy between the perceptions of an individual faculty number and his or her colleagues? This might occur in those areas where diversity is an individual priority but not a major concern for the academic department (e.g., items 9, 11, 12, and 13).

Questions That Shape the Diversity Discussion with Faculty

In addition to survey responses, faculty can provide their perspective or feedback on diversity by responding to probing questions in focus groups or as individuals. The questions could be distributed across categories in the following manner:

Faculty Values

1. What is faculty's ethical responsibility concerning diversity and the discipline-based curriculum?
2. What is the intrinsic and extrinsic value of diversity to faculty?
3. Does diversity conflict with any values in your department or program?

Diverse Student Populations

1. How would faculty judge the success of diversity programs for different populations in particular classes or across certain learning environments?

2. Do diverse students use academic supports such as tutoring in the most effective ways?
3. Do student demographics affect how you deliver your course content?
4. What information about student subpopulations (women, athletes, students of color, nontraditional students, etc.) do student support personnel use. And how can this information benefit faculty work?

Classroom and Curricular Factors

1. What is the social and structural environment of a course, and how does it affect the performance of different populations?
2. What is the importance of putting what we teach in the classroom into historical and political perspectives?
3. Are you familiar with the best research and practices associated with learning communities?

Structural Considerations

1. How do we create educational structures and environments that allow students to try diverse experiences?
2. Can we align in-class and out-of-class experiences to promote equitable learning outcomes for diverse learners?
3. Are faculty development efforts structured in a way that benefits faculty?

Outcomes (Academic and Skill-Related)

1. What skills should we teach students so they can live and function effectively in a pluralistic society?
2. In what courses is it necessary to assess student learning outcomes in terms of diversity?
3. Do your instructional practices reflect learning outcomes associated with your course?

As mentioned earlier faculty buy-in for diversity may be limited because they don't associate the concept with traditional work they value. Therefore, it is important that any coupling of diversity with fundamental faculty concerns or business be perceived as maintaining and, when appropriate, enhancing fundamental areas of importance. For example, a very fundamental assessment question might be: "What are your teaching goals for a particular course?" Diversity considerations allow that question to be expanded to read: "What are your teaching goals for a particular course for students who are diverse in skill level, age, race, culture, class, and/or gender?" The second question clearly demands some focus on a student-centered model of learning. A comparable question for professional schools and health-related programs might be: "As you think about the changing demographics of your client populations, what do you need to incorporate into the clinical training component of the health care program?" Community colleges would frame a question that accounts for the open-enrollment aspect of their mission: "Describe how faculty use instructional approaches for older students, commuters, and those who are less skilled or at risk?"

Discussion about diversity as a scholarly activity can find a parallel with Huber and Hutchings's (2005) argument that knowledge workers and lifelong learners need "pedagogical intelligence," which allows others to construct for themselves (and sometimes for others) activities that allow learning, growth, and change. This capacity is important because of the transformation that is occurring due to changing enrollment patterns, in the ways that technology and globalization affect teaching practices and the discipline, and in the shifting conditions of knowledge itself, especially socially constructed knowledge, that is, knowledge that emerges from social interactions, social perceptions, and the belief systems of those who control the dissemination of knowledge.

Huber and Hutchings contend that the momentum that has pushed us to discuss what is needed to produce "pedagogical thinkers" cannot be sustained without continued leadership and commitment from many areas. They mention five areas of action that promise to yield significant benefits. I contend that, because of the similarities between a discussion of the scholarship of teaching and learning and the scholarship of diversity, the same action areas would be appropriate:

1. There is a need to establish the structures and occasions when people from different areas of campus can come together for sustained, substantive, and constructive discussion about diversity, particularly how to conceptualize and implement it.

2. Students need to be part of the discussion about diversity, and they need multiple venues to think and talk together to others inside and

outside the academy. They also need to stay within the parameters and ground rules for critical discourse or they will limit their chances of meta-thinking, or linking related concepts, about diversity.

3. Diversity work needs to be addressed in a format that allows it to be perceived as serious, intellectual work. As I argue in this book, there must be concrete evidence that diversity has an impact on other areas of serious intellectual work, that is, teaching, learning, and research.

4. Documentation of diversity work must be advanced with new genres and forms to serve as a teaching tool for others, to disseminate more widely, and to begin collecting and archiving the success stories.

5. Higher education in general and colleges and universities in particular should help to build and maintain the infrastructure needed to make high-quality diversity work available and accessible to all. The scholarship of teaching and learning and of diversity belongs in the public domain and should not be confined by intellectual property rights, privatization, or commercialization. In some cases asking research questions about the quality and productivity of on-campus diversity efforts can elevate those outcomes to a scholarly level.

Competing Faculty Perspectives

While faculty may have positive or negative beliefs about diversity and its place in the academy, the reality is that their beliefs, perceptions, and values are complex. Their responses to one question might elicit a particular response (positive or negative), while a related question might produce more varied reactions to the concept of diversity. Perhaps the context in which a question is framed or understood is important. How relevant or familiar questions or choices may be to faculty respondents might also be a factor.

Figure 3.2 attempts to elicit faculty views on diversity outcomes across four areas: academic reputation, value to the discipline, legitimacy, and competing interests.

Faculty may not be responsive to diversity-related assessment if there is little evidence of previous attempts to survey their values and attitudes about topics they feel more comfortable discussing. Faculty are not oblivious to the politics of the diversity discussion, so their receptiveness to such discussions must take the politics into account.

FIGURE 3.2
Faculty Views on Diversity-Related Outcomes

Instructions: Please check any of the boxes which apply for each outcome

Outcomes	Could enhance the academic reputation		Is important to the discipline		Has perceived legitimacy to my faculty colleagues		May be competing with department concerns	
	YES	NO	YES	NO	YES	NO	YES	NO
1. Curricular transformation	☐	☐	☐	☐	☐	☐	☐	☐
2. Recruitment of diverse faculty	☐	☐	☐	☐	☐	☐	☐	☐
3. Develop new teaching methods for diverse learners	☐	☐	☐	☐	☐	☐	☐	☐
4. Added training on diversity for professional programs	☐	☐	☐	☐	☐	☐	☐	☐
5. Development of diverse scholarship	☐	☐	☐	☐	☐	☐	☐	☐
6. Development of applied and theoretical model	☐	☐	☐	☐	☐	☐	☐	☐
7. Research with multicultural dimensions	☐	☐	☐	☐	☐	☐	☐	☐
8. Enhancement of a diverse Classroom Community	☐	☐	☐	☐	☐	☐	☐	☐

Faculty Development: Finding Effective Strategies

What might be the best-case scenario concerning faculty involvement in projects that facilitate teaching and learning in the diverse classroom? It might involve a large number of faculty from different disciplines meeting monthly to discuss such topics as the definition of diversity, how course content and teaching practices can be transformed for diversity, how to assess outcomes of curricular and pedagogical change, and diverse teaching and learning styles. Unfortunately, the reality is that faculty participation in such development projects varies across campuses and often involves too few people. What often emerges is a smaller core group of loyal practitioners.

In the early stages of the project development, each campus should select those strategies that can reach more potential participants. The following strategies may be valuable:

1. Recognize time demands—participation in faculty development efforts requires significant time and may compete with other demands. It may be more attractive to offer several levels or categories of participation that entail varying amounts of commitment. If resources are available, an attractive incentive might be to offer summer seminars or one semester of release time.

2. An apprentice model—some faculty may be more amenable to mentoring by a respected colleague in a realistic setting, than to learning in a simulated format. Mentors should have developed a repertoire of successful skill sets and be able to communicate effectively with their colleagues.

3. Faculty community—certain imperatives have the ability to drag other imperatives along. An institutional initiative to develop a faculty community that promotes diversity outcomes might inspire a growing pool of faculty—especially if they recognize a linkage to other imperatives they value.

4. Creative recruiting—traditional recruiting strategies, such as word-of-mouth, offering incentives, and formal announcements, can be effective seminal tools. However, a faculty development effort that is associated with an academy of scholars could carry significantly more prestige than one that has less visibility.

5. Outcome-based emphasis—a combination of strategies 3 and 4 above

could lead to a faculty community of scholars whose focus is on diversity-related outcomes, such as:

- To examine the relationship among instructional styles and varied learning styles
- To understand the fundamental relationship among effective teaching, learning outcomes, and diversity among different student populations
- To explore in a practical way how faculty can produce more equitable outcomes in the classroom when students exhibit disparate needs
- To identify the student learning outcomes and associated strategies that instructors should expect from applying diversity in the classroom

6. Strengthening traditional outcomes—academic departments might respond to diversity efforts that strengthen the department's traditional goals in response to regional accreditation. At a research institution grant productivity could be enhanced by the application of diversity to the proposal. On the other hand, a comprehensive university might need to strengthen its general education requirements. A community college might want to enhance the completion rates of racially diverse students in a particular certificate program or increase the percentage of diverse students who transition successfully into the workforce.

Multicultural Classroom Resource Guide: IUPUI's Electronic Accessory for Faculty Development

The 21st century has been identified as a time when people expect to access and use information in real time. As the portals and avenues that facilitate cyberexploration grow exponentially, the issue becomes how we reduce the avalanche of available resource information to a workable, useful cache.

In the case of faculty who want to enhance both their knowledge base and competencies on teaching in the multicultural classroom, a very valuable tool has emerged that can advance the efforts of an individual faculty member, an academic department, a center for teaching and learning, etc. That tool is the Multicultural Classroom Resource Guide, housed at Indiana

University-Purdue University Indianapolis (IUPUI), which can be accessed at http://opd.iupui.edu/ompd/guide/.

In higher education initiatives are often launched that are timely, address an obvious need, understand their place as a seminal piece of work (as opposed to a finished product), and ultimately serve as a catalyst for others to replicate and improve on. Despite their creative emergence, such seminal initiatives also run the risk of bearing the brunt of constructive critiques. However, certain efforts are destined to succeed because they are grounded in scholarly inquiry, they are sustained by broad team efforts, and they address topics that relate to the goals and priorities of institutions.

What Is the Resource Guide?

In May–June 2000 at IUPUI, the concerns of several groups led to critical discussions about retention and success of first-generation students, particularly those belonging to racial and ethnic minorities. As a foundation for several emerging initiatives on the campus, a review of all relevant literature was conducted to generate an internal clearinghouse of information accessible to all concerned members of the university community. Several organizations seized on this opportunity to channel the wealth of available information into an online Multicultural Classroom Resource Guide.

The Resource Guide includes information extracted from books, chapters, articles, and online materials. The electronic format of the Guide makes it available to an expanding audience of users who can take advantage of various organizational formats and multiple links.

The topical emphasis of the Resource Guide is on diversity, but it does not address the concept in a general way. The specific focus is on the multicultural classroom, and the target audience is faculty. As I indicated earlier, the Guide is a seminal effort that will continue to expand and improve. The online Guide, accompanied by an information booklet that contains a history of development and a statement of purpose, provides readers with a general idea of its organization, layout, and content.

General Strengths of the Resource Guide

Most users will see the Web site as a way to search for resources (written materials and research efforts) about diversity and the multicultural classroom. The search can be conducted in a variety of ways, and it provides the feel that one is walking through a library. For example, identified resources are accompanied by brief abstracts. Although the number of available resources varies dramatically among topics, most researchers will find what is available to be sufficient and in many cases provocative.

The Topical Selections, or major headings, are in line with those one would expect to see on the subject of the multicultural classroom:

- Diversity and Multicultural Education: General Issues
- The Classroom: Reasons for Multicultural Course Transformation
- The Faculty
- Students
- Curriculum: Issues of Content
- Issues of Pedagogy
- Change Management
- University Environment: Beyond the Classroom

Visitors to the site can proceed directly to the Topical Outline by clicking on that link or a similar link that appears on other Web pages. Of special value is the fact that the outline includes subtopical areas with author, date, and links to an annotated bibliography.

The site offers a redesigned welcome center with streamlined links to the main guide content. The center offers a very clear categorical breakdown and opportunity to search topics. There do not appear to be any accessibility issues associated with this page.

The Main Guide Page has navigation options that include specific populations, academic disciplines, and IUPUI's Course Transformation Model. Recognizing that the concept of diversity embraces many populations, the link to populations accounts for race, culture, gender, sexual orientation, and religion.

The Guide can serve as a scholarly resource for young faculty who must develop a research portfolio, and it can facilitate the work of faculty groups that evaluate teaching, assess learning, revise general education curriculums, and attempt to address current education realities.

One of the most valuable components of the Resource Guide is the On-Line Resource Submission Form, which offers site visitors the opportunity to add to the existing information base. The developers of the Resource

Guide desire to share their expertise with a broad audience while asking users to take a vested interest in the development of this important tool. A modified example of a similar resource guide would be a worthy addition to the diversity efforts on many campuses. There are few excuses for not attempting to structure some type of coherent toolbox for faculty use.

Faculty Development and Diversity: The Annual IUPUI Symposium Highlighting the Research and Teaching of Faculty, Staff, and Students of Color

At IUPUI, the Office for Multicultural Professional Development (OMPD) is charged with facilitating retention of less-represented faculty on campus; this is partially accomplished through coordinating and sponsoring community-building events and, more specifically, by creating venues to highlight the work of faculty of color on campus. OMPD's work ensures that diversity is represented not only as a scholarly activity but also as a functional part of the teaching, learning, and research paradigm.

Dr. Sherree Wilson, appointed special assistant to the chancellor at IUPUI in January 2005 and founding director of OMPD from 2001 to 2004, provides the following summary of the development and impact of the office.

> Since the spring, 2000 OMPD has sponsored and coordinated the annual IUPUI Symposium Highlighting the Research of Faculty, Staff and Students of Color. The idea for the Symposium was first suggested in 1999 by a faculty advisory group to the staff in the Office for Minority Faculty Development (changed to OMPD in 2001). The committee suggested that an event be held which would feature and showcase the scholarly and creative activities of faculty of color at IUPUI. It was later agreed that participation in the Symposium should not be limited to faculty, but rather staff and students should also be encouraged to present their work. In particular, the participation by students was viewed as a way for them to hone their research skills, work one-on-one with faculty members to develop and refine specific research projects, and encourage students to consider academic career options. Faculty also began to explore how teaching could facilitate the development of student competencies,
>
> The first step for Symposium participation is proposal submission; potential presenters are required to develop and submit proposals for review

and acceptance. Any student who wishes to submit a proposal is required to work with a faculty member who advises the student on the proposal writing and presentation process. Presentations are either delivered orally or as posters, and presenters represent a wide range of disciplines including the sciences, health care, social work, the arts, education and humanities. The Symposium also features keynote speakers, general faculty or administrators from the institution.

The IUPUI Symposium serves to enhance diversity on campus by: fostering the retention of faculty of color, and encouraging their professional development. Moody (2004) suggested that in order to facilitate the retention of less represented faculty, institutions should: (1) sponsor career-development workshops and community-building events; (2) encourage and develop senior faculty to serve as champions for diversity; and (3) help new faculty make scholarly connections within and outside their departments. Additionally, the Symposium addresses another component of the campus' mission: excellence in teaching and learning.

The IUPUI Symposium brings faculty, staff and students of color together for an event that not only celebrates scholarly accomplishments but also helps to build community among the participants. Proponents of critical race theory (Delgado & Stefanic, 2001; Solórzano, Ceja, & Yosso, 2000; Villalpando & Delgado Bernal, 2002) speak to the importance of counter-spaces on predominantly White campuses. Counterspaces are sites or locations, and in the case of the Symposium, events that promote a positive racial climate among persons of color by providing nurturing and supportive environments to individuals who share common experiences.

The Symposium organizers also regularly encourage new or junior faculty to submit proposals for the event; this provides a venue for the faculty to meet and interact with senior faculty and receive feedback on their research. Additionally, some participants have established research collaborations with faculty colleagues and/or developed mentoring relationships with senior faculty as a result of their participation in the Symposium. Senior faculty are also enlisted to serve as session moderators, and include majority faculty as well as faculty of color. Through their participation, the faculty demonstrate their support of the event as well as their commitment to advancing and promoting faculty diversity on campus.

The Symposium facilitates excellence in teaching and learning in a number of ways for students and faculty. For some student participants, the Symposium serves as their first presentation experience where they develop and refine their presentation skills and also learn the ways that academic professionals share ideas. Secondly, the requirement that students work with faculty sponsors to develop their proposals and subsequent presentations helps to establish mentoring relationships which expose students to a significant aspect of faculty work life as well as faculty role models; the students may also consider enrolling in graduate school and pursuing careers in academia. Next, faculty who observe the successful faculty-student interactions may be encouraged to consider implementing and using this alternative teaching method by developing similar research partnerships. Finally, faculty who hear and learn more about the topics presented during the Symposium may elect to incorporate the ideas into their teaching thereby helping to transform the curriculum. It is evident that the IUPUI symposium reaches far beyond simply the identification of a place for faculty development and instead represents a multi-pronged initiative that is productive, sustainable, scholarly, public and rewarding to varied participants.

Diversity as an Attractive Incentive to Academic Departments

The IUPUI model is a strategic tool that can arouse the consciousness of a campus by providing much-needed exposure to nontraditional and/or complementary scholarship, research, and pedagogic expertise. In a phase-development model, it represents the seminal stages of penetration into the campus culture. The important short- and long-term gains depend on our ability to encourage faculty ownership of diversity initiatives. The challenge, then, is to package diversity as an attractive incentive.

The following seven areas are closely tied to existing faculty values and incentives. In subsequent chapters I discuss several of these in terms of their importance for implementing diversity. Diversity becomes an attractive incentive:

1. when it is connected to strengthening the curriculum (general education, first-year seminars, diversity requirements, etc.);
2. when it assumes a core identity among new/existing majors/minors/concentrations/graduate programs;
3. when it strengthens the tradition of international education, globalism, and study abroad;
4. when it contributes to quality and uniformity across interdisciplinary areas;

5. when it promotes an analysis of the discipline and of scholarship;
6. when it transforms how faculty think about themselves, their research, and their teaching (an evolving diverse faculty community); and
7. when it contributes to the research agenda of individual faculty or the department.

Faculty generally do not perceive diversity activities rooted in nonacademic areas, such as student affairs, as rigorous. The academic mission of a college or university takes primacy over all else, and our diversity efforts should reflect its place of importance. This does not suggest that little attention should be given to cocurricular efforts that support diversity, rather that we should recognize that their impact is often short term, unless they are linked to academic concerns.

Challenging the Borders of the Academy

The sustained discussion of diversity as a political concept, a demographic indicator, an aspect of climate, a structural framework, and so on limits its acceptance as one of the potential frontiers of innovation in the academy. When it is associated with three cornerstones of the academy (pedagogy, curriculum, and learning), diversity can realize the same shared goals as interdisciplinary programs: to reconfigure the social and cognitive space of the academy into a new community of pluralities that's both intercultural and interdisciplinary (Humphreys, 1997).

Reflecting on the complexity of a rapidly changing society and the need to adapt to change, campus leaders must encourage serious discussion about the new academy that can inspire an introspective look at how their institutions accept and legitimize diversity. There is an urgent need to elevate the discussion so that the desired outcomes associated with diversity are viewed as aligned with the outcomes in other valued areas. For example, diversity outcomes that are academic in nature can parallel outcomes that are associated with interdisciplinary programs (Klein, 1999, pp. 18–19):

- greater tolerance of ambiguity and paradox
- sensitivity to ethical dimensions of issues
- ability to synthesize or integrate

- ability to demythologize experts
- humility and sensitivity to bias
- enlarged perspectives or horizons
- critical and unconventional thinking
- empowerment
- creativity and original insights
- ability to balance subjective and objective thinking

The proponents of inclusion, that is, those who want to diversify the curriculum, must come to the same conclusion as the Association for Integrative Studies: an examination of learning claims and desired outcomes strongly suggests that process, not content, is the primary focus. Thus pedagogy and faculty development assume a more significant role in our discussion about the new academy and diversity's place within it.

Organizational Change Is Intentional and Systematic

While serving as the director of the Office of Faculties and TA (Teaching Assistant) Development at the Ohio State University, Nancy Van Nate Chism led the effort to "institutionalize" inclusive pedagogical practices and curricular development. Starting from the premise that faculty and students bring with them to the college learning environment biases that permeate their respective societies, she suggests that looking critically at frank consideration of factors that constrain inclusive education practices is a crucial first step toward change (Chism, 1995).

Discussions about the debilitating consequences of narrow curriculum choices and pedagogy often limit themselves to the real and perceived impact on underrepresented or diverse students. More attention needs to be paid to the prospect of deficit-based learning of majority students or the impact of scholarship in an academic discipline. As Chism (1995, p. 329) notes: "Failing to be inclusive with respect to curriculum issues results in narrow scholarship, and second in the loss of potential new scholars." In other words, a panoramic perspective must involve well-planned, systematic, intentional, and goal-oriented organizational change. Chism suggests three distinct phases that should evolve at colleges/universities that desire change in curriculum or pedagogy (p. 335):

I. The Preparation Phase

For example: Conduct careful research and analyses to identify and define the problem clearly. Follow the assessment by formulating an action plan. Propose the plan to appropriate campus constituents (internal and external), weigh their feedback, and include appropriate revisions.

II. Planning According to Institutional Characteristics

For example: Planning must respect and be guided by the organizational structure and authority of academic and administrative governance. The relative strength of different groups relative to governance varies across institutions.

III. The Implementation Phase

For example: Appoint a committee to build and present the case for implementing the plan that will use a range of information, data, and feedback as it facilitates "meaning-making" for the campus community.

Much is at stake when an institution attempts to implement organizational change in areas that have strong traditional grounding. Any planning process must assure faculty and students that an inclusive educational environment elevates the most valued aspects of the teaching, learning, and research process. Moreover, an incremental or phase-driven model will be palatable to a wider range of audiences and will allow for corrections at each phase before moving forward. Those who support a diversity agenda generally want to move faster than those who are neutral, but the allies of diversity and globalism must recognize that pace is not the sole priority. It is the appropriate balance among pace, process, and excellence that will elevate efforts to make diversity and globalism a successful institutional initiative.

Organizational Change and the Inevitability of Conflict

More often than not discussions about diversity and globalism on a college campus may be unfamiliar to students. Faculty responsibility for equitable classrooms suggests a level of expertise and preparedness that reflects the need to introduce students to the conditions for effective learning, reduce the real or perceived status differential between teacher and student and between students, and alert students to their responsibility to one another especially under conditions of ambiguity or tension.

Anderson (1999) suggests that most faculty are not prepared to promote effective social arrangements or alliances within the classroom, primarily because their own academic training has given them little opportunity to develop expertise in this area. Thus, they are often left to engage in avoidance behaviors or to reconstruct the ideal learning environments that they remember from their own past, or in the case of many part-time faculty, they attempt to transfer the mechanics of the professional workplace to the classroom. Goodman (1995) discusses a framework for diverse college classrooms, where the potential for difficult dialogues is pronounced. She suggests that instructors use a model of social identity development that explores each individual's way of viewing the world and himself or herself as a member of a social alliance. Such a model is appropriate for majority and underrepresented students, those who are advantaged and those who are not. The goal of the model, which uses five developmental stages, is to help students and the instructor make sense of different reactions and perspectives.

Why are concepts such as "social identity" and "social arrangements" so important to inclusive teaching? What do they imply that is missing in teacher-student and student-student interactions in the classroom? How does incorporating such concepts into faculty considerations bring about changes in pedagogy and classroom structure? When students arrive at college, they have preconceived notions of what constitutes effective classroom discussions and interactions, but such beliefs are not based on realistic experiences. Moreover, many have not faced the challenge of engaging other students and faculty who do not agree with them and who may be different from them on one or more demographic characteristics. For many students, interacting with their peers in social settings outside of class is nowhere near as threatening as revealing what they really think about important and/or controversial topics. Many instructors are unsure of (a) the steps necessary to facilitate engaged classroom dialogue; (b) how their identity as teaching faculty can serve as a positive cue for student interactions; and (c) how the social relations of students in and out of the classroom facilitate their learning and engagement.

Mooney, Fordham, and Lehr (2005) discuss the implementation of a faculty development program to promote civil and classroom discourse by using writing and oral communication skill development at St. Lawrence University. The Oral Communication Institute (OCI) affords faculty the opportunity to reflect on how their classrooms can become communication environments, and how the social identities of students might influence how students communicate in the classroom. A core OCI belief is that engaged conversations between faculty will develop both individual and group outcomes just as they do when such conversations are encouraged between students.

The University of Washington fostered both identity development and social relations among students and faculty members as part of an annual seminar or summer institute on curricular transformation (Schmitz & Taranath, 2005). During the seminar, both groups examine new theories and pedagogies, engage in contentious discussions, and rethink the development of various courses. Among the issues covered are: how to establish one's own positionality in the classroom; how to deal with tension; how to deal with student resistance to new world views and perspectives, and how to deal with an incident of bias or prejudice in the classroom. Faculty report that attending the seminar alters the traditional university structure in which they are framed as experts in their field and allows them to reconstruct their identities as students in a larger conversation about social differences and pedagogy.

Difficult dialogues and conflict are inevitable when diversity and globalism demand organizational change, especially when very traditional values have supported an organizational structure. With this in mind, there is an alternative to a reactive or defensive position—training, preparation, courage, and a renewed commitment to educational equity and excellence. To some degree, the behavioral standards students exhibit in the classroom are extensions of their standards outside it and are also shaped by the cues provided by the instructor about the nature of the social arrangement in the classroom. Faculty roles and responsibilities concerning appropriate and inappropriate behavior in the classroom should not be perceived as an imposition by some outside force; rather, they should be viewed and valued as a natural extension of the learning process.

References

Anderson, J. (1999, Spring). Faculty responsibility for promoting conflict-free college classrooms. *New Directions for Teaching and Learning, (77),* 69–76.

Chism, N. (1995). Promoting inclusiveness in college teaching. In W. A. Wright (Ed.), *Teaching improvement practices* (pp. 325–345). Bolton, MA: Anker Publishing.

Delgado, R., & Stefanic, J. (2001). *Critical race theory: An introduction.* New York: NYU Press.

Goodman, D. (1995). Difficult dialogues: Enhancing discussions about diversity. *College Teaching, 43*(2), 47–52.

Huber, M. T., & Hutchings, P. (2005). *The advancement of learning: Building the teaching commons.* Stanford, CA: Carnegie Foundation for the Advancement of Teaching.

Humphreys, D. (1997). *General education and American commitments: A national report on diversity courses and requirements.* Washington, DC: American Association of Colleges and Universities.

Indiana University Fact Book (2003). Gender and ethnic group of faculty. Bloomington, IN: University Budget Office. Retrieved from http://factbook.in diana.edu/fbook03/fbindx03.html.

Indiana University Reporting & Research. (2004). *Official enrollment report, 14*(1) Bloomington, IN: University Budget Office. Retrieved from www.indiana.edu/ ~urr/enrollment/2004-5/enrollmentsummary4048.pdf.

Klein, J. T. (1999). *Mapping interdisciplinary studies. A discussion paper for faculty members and academic leaders.* Washington, DC: American Association of Colleges and Universities.

Moody, J. (2004). *Faculty diversity: Problems and solutions.* New York: Routledge-Falmer Press.

Mooney, K. M., Fordham, T., & Lehr, V. D. (2005). A faculty development program to promote engaged classroom dialogue: The Oral Communication Institute. *To Improve the Academy, 23.* Boston: Anker Publishing.

Schmitz, B., & Taranath, A. (2005). Positionality and authority in curriculum transformation: Faculty/student collaboration in course design. In M. L. Ouellett (Ed.), *Teaching inclusively* (pp. 105–110). Stillwater, OK: New Forums.

Solórzano, D. G., Ceja, M., & Yosso, T. (2000). Critical race theory, racial microgressions, and campus racial climate: The experiences of African American college students. *Journal of Negro Education, 69*(1/2), 60–73.

Villalpando, O., & Delgato Bernal, D. (2002). A critical race theory analysis of barriers that impede the success of faculty of color. In W. A. Smith, P. G. Altbach, & K. Lomotey (Eds.), *The racial crisis in American higher education: Continuing challenges for the twenty-first century* (2nd ed., pp. 243–279). Albany, NY: SUNY Press.

4

ACCOUNTING FOR DIVERSITY WITHIN THE TEACHING AND LEARNING PARADIGM

M any members of the academy contend that what they value most is reflected in the (a) curricular content they select, (b) the pedagogy they choose to use, and (c) the research and scholarship they pursue. While differences exist in the attention or emphasis on each area and how quality is defined, one of the major products of faculty's efforts is the impact on student learning. How does incorporating diversity into the discussion about traditional ways of teaching and the learning experience reshape that discussion? If one were to argue that faculty have an ethical responsibility to address diversity in the classroom, how receptive would faculty be to such an expectation? How can faculty concerns about diversity's impact on academic freedom be addressed while also trying to depoliticize the discourse? Such important questions and considerations should be addressed in the early stages of conversation and should preempt any attempts at implementation.

Among the supporters of a redesigned teaching and learning paradigm are those who point to the challenge of a rapidly growing diverse student population. According to the National Center for Educational Statistics, between 1976 and 2000, the proportion of American college students from minority groups nearly doubled, increasing from 15 percent to 28 percent; the greatest increase is among Hispanic students (Lampkin, 2004). Of greater significance is that many of these students are first-generation college and university students and exhibit some of the factors associated with being at risk and/or unfamiliar with the cultural expectations of college. These cohorts generally enroll in community colleges, minority-serving institutions, proprietary schools, less-selective four year institutions, and distance education programs.

Several national and regional initiatives, have evolved that target the success rates of underserved and underrepresented groups. One example of a well-developed initiative is "Achieving the Dream: Community Colleges Count," funded by the Lumina Foundation. In summer 2004, 27 community colleges in five states became foundation project sites. Although the global program's objective is to maintain access for students, the specific outcomes are affected by the degree to which diversity is accounted for in the campus-based model of teaching and learning. The goal of the Lumina grant is to increase the percentage of students who:

- complete remedial/developmental courses and move into general curriculum courses;
- complete "gatekeeper courses"—those that are particularly troublesome for many students and that have consistently high failure and withdrawal rates;
- complete courses with a grade of "C" or higher;
- persist from one semester to the next; and
- earn certificates and degrees and/or transfer to four-year institutions.

It is difficult to imagine how these outcomes would occur without a faculty commitment to apply a diversity-enriched model of effective teaching. Sternberg (2005) contends that when students from challenged backgrounds do not receive instruction that takes into account the diversity of their needs and abilities, we run the risk of creating an academic underclass that underachieves. He is one of the few researchers who posit a direct link between the access of underrepresented groups in colleges and universities and the type of teaching needed to facilitate their success and retention. According to Sternberg's theory of multiple intelligences, one must assess a broader range of skills among diverse learners. For example, he adds assessment of creative and practical skills to the more traditional assessment of analytical and memory skills.

In his discussion of group differences and learning styles, Anderson (1988) proposes that certain populations use the affective dimension as a significant filter as they process, organize, and synthesize information in their environment. He suggests that this is more characteristic of cultures that place more value on the presence and use of the affective dimension. In a formal learning environment such as a college classroom, learners exhibit a propensity to make personal and subjective evaluations of the information to be learned, how it is presented in the text, and about the instructor. The presence of diverse characteristics or demographics associated with this type of learning style often predisposes students to minimize the stated expectations of the instructor while they construct meaning relative to their own reality or way of knowing. In other words, students personalize learning in ways that may or may not promote actual learning and, in many cases, may jeopardize their chance for success in the course.

Why does such a predisposition emerge across some groups and not others? Ortiz (2000) suggests that the relationship between culture and worldview contributes to what we value, what we learn to value, and how we understand the world in both concrete and abstract forms. She suggests that this connection is so "close and direct" that people are generally unaware of its influences. Moreover, diverse students perceive knowledge and truth as contextual as opposed to absolute. In the college classroom, diverse backgrounds, skill levels, perspectives, and worldviews have become the norm and not the exception. The challenge for instructors is to recognize the needs and rights of contextual learners, and to create equitable learning environments that allow them to find their place in the academy.

The notion that students contextualize the learning environment and construct their own versions of the meaning of knowledge and curricular content is fundamental to several models of learning. In his classic work on the intellectual and ethical development of college students, Perry (1970) presents a stage development model of how individuals actively construct their own reality.

Robert Kegan (1982) refers to Perry's conceptualization as "meaning-making" (p. 2), a developmental process that is systematic and longitudinal—it evolves over the person's life span. One could move through six holistic stages or forms of meaning-making with each form affecting how a person perceives reality. Kegan contends that the expectations for learning in the college classroom don't always match where students are developmentally in their preferred meaning-making. Ignelzi (2000) notes that meaning-making is not the same thing as intellectual potential or ability (p. 10). Meaning-making refers to how individuals learn over time to process, interpret, and organize information related to their experience. Learning difficulties, especially for diverse students, may not be the result of learning deficits. Instead, they may reflect incongruence between the educational expectations of the instructor and the students' position on a meaning-making continuum.

Meaning-Making and the Diversity of Race and Gender

While theories of racial and gender identity often emphasize how individuals are socialized into membership groups, such identity theories also suggest how various identities influence how people interpret their experience across different contexts and ultimately make evaluative judgments based on this feedback. In other words, racial and gender identity become critical components of meaning-making.

Extrapolating from models of multicultural and multiracial counseling, Carter (1995) and Ponterotto, Casas, Suzuki, and Alexander (1995) suggest that racial identity affects how one forms perceptions and processes information. Instructors who are unfamiliar with or unaware of the relationship of racial and cultural identity to the learning process may devalue the intellectual process that is affirmed by diverse groups, especially students of color. As Magolda (2000, p. 94) indicates so astutely, "Expressing openness to learning about and respecting students' experiences can create opportunities to hear how their unique experiences affect their learning."

Gender identity development and sexual orientation also evolve as complex processes that are mediated by experiences, environments, and motivational factors. When female students in college settings are not validated and supported and are assigned a secondary status, their motivation to learn declines. In some cases, they begin to question their abilities, decision-making skills, goals, and choices of career.

The landmark work of Belenky and her colleagues (1986) outlines the disconnection that women experience in college classrooms when pedagogical applications are at odds with the stages of cognitive development in women. Other authors have described the impact that social forces have on women's beliefs, attitudes, and performance (Eccles & Jacobs, 1987). Clinchy, Belenky, Goldberger, and Torule (1985) and Webb (1995) discuss the value of "connecting" education to the experiences, learning preferences, modes of interaction, cognitive styles, etc., of women. Although much of the seminal work on gender, identity development, and success in the college classroom evolved in the 1980s, it received renewed attention when the president of Harvard University, Laurence H. Summers, suggested that innate gender differences account for the absence of women in science, math, and engineering (*Chronicle of Higher Education*, March 4, 2005, p. 1).

Ayers-Nachamkin (1992) discovered that her initial perceptions about student difficulty in an introductory statistics course (math anxiety) could be rechanneled into a set of proactive principles that encouraged empowerment of students as learners. While she personally identifies her approach as having its roots in her feminist consciousness, the generic applicability of her methods translates into an alternate pedagogy that benefits all students. One turning point in the curricular change and diversity process occurred in the last decade as authors, scholars, and researchers have sought to address scientific literacy for women. *Gender, Science, and the Undergraduate Curriculum* (Musil, 2001) summarizes a fundamental position of all of the chapter's authors: a critical examination of curricular change in the sciences must be done against a backdrop of women's studies and feminist pedagogical theory.

Anxiety Among Nontraditional Learners

In March 1989, at Tacoma Community College (TCC), Karen Clark and Kathy Acker submitted a proposal to offer a course on an experimental basis, titled "Overcoming Math Anxiety"—a coordinated study of Math 88 and HR 98. As an open-admissions institution, TCC confronts the common challenge of addressing the needs of diverse learners in the college classroom. In this case two instructors sought to focus on a consistent problem of many returning adult students—math avoidance.

The proposed course focused on students of varying ages, skill levels, genders, and in some instances race and culture. These students often delayed taking math because of inadequate preparation early in their academic careers, traumatic experiences with math, and/or an excessive time lapse since last encountering math. The resulting barrier is not just academic, but psychological as well. The fundamental premise of the course was that integrating a math anxiety component was needed, but it must be taught in the context of the skills and content of the actual course.

The sequence of events that occur throughout the course is as follows:

1. Establish a sense of group identity—students are encouraged to see themselves as a collaborative group whose members share a common goal—success in the course. Individual anxiety is tempered when everyone in the group shares a similar fear. More important, poor performance carries no stigma, nor does it imply negative attributions about individual or group characteristics.

2. Develop an autobiography of math anxiety—students are asked to chronicle the feelings, perceptions, and events associated with their anxiety about math. This exercise helps them to think about their anxiety in objective ways and to analyze, perhaps for the first time, why it developed.

3. Express negative feelings—students are asked to write down their own negative feelings about math, especially the relationship between their expectations and outcomes. They are then introduced to two techniques: (a) thought stopping and (b) neurolinguistic variety—students say negative statements in different ways: loudly, softly, angrily, fearfully, etc.

4. Practice self-talk—as students do homework, they talk themselves through the exercise. They solve problems on one sheet of paper and write their self-talk on another. In this way, students can analyze where their conceptual roadblocks are occurring in a language that is familiar to them.

5. Adhere to formal standards of classroom behavior—students are given two important documents that relate to math anxiety: a bill of rights and a code of responsibilities. Thus they have a voice in setting expectations and they learn what is expected of them.

6. Practice a relaxation exercise—three weeks into the course, students are introduced to breathing techniques, mental rehearsal, and the use of affirmations (silently repeating statements such as, "I am capable," "I am powerful," and "I have the confidence and ability to do this.")

While a skeptic might suggest that this represents a "guru-ish" or transcendental approach to teaching and learning math, it is evident that the instructors are addressing the three core areas often associated with anxiety: emotion, cognition, and behavior. Moreover, their strategies represent a student-centered approach to teaching and individual empowerment.

The course is a concrete example of the impact of teaching for "retention," that is, targeting specific outcomes (affective development, student-student engagement, grade performance, and better comprehension of abstract course content). Among the student outcomes addressed are enhancing students' attitude toward learning, their expectations for success, and their academic self-esteem. All of these factors are identified in the retention research as correlates of student success and retention. An open-admissions institution like Takoma Community College often must rely on innovative pedagogies that are tailored to the needs and characteristics of the diverse populations they serve.

In terms of assessment, the instructor compared the progress of students in these sections to that of students in similar sections without math avoidance strategies. They also tracked students longitudinally in successive math classes. Finally, the students responded to surveys that examined their attitude toward math and any changes in career plans based on math.

The Teaching-Learning Project at Miami-Dade Community College: Faculty Instructional Seminars

The previous example used a course-based approach to address a critical problem encountered by many students from diverse backgrounds. It is important that faculty continue to address comparable situations and to be supported in this by their respective institutions. However, the most significant impact on faculty and students occurs when faculty can benefit from a well-designed and -supported, comprehensive, and systematic initiative. One example of a project initiative with such characteristics occurred at Miami-Dade Community College during the tenure of former president Robert McCabe. Few presidents exhibited the vision, passion, and commitment to their institution and especially their students as did McCabe, and the college has continued to maintain its legacy of student-centered excellence and to serve as an external benchmark for two-year (and some four-year) institutions.

Miami-Dade CC provided its faculty with a series of instructional seminars that allowed them, over time, to hone their instructional skills to meet the needs of their students. A core group of faculty emerged whose members had been identified previously as exceptional and promising instructors. The following represents the structural outline that was developed for the curriculum:

I. Theoretical Base

- Theories of teaching/learning
- Traditional approaches to teaching/learning
- Nontraditional approaches to teaching/learning

II. Course Planning

- Analyzing, sequencing, pacing
- Developing interesting and effective materials
- Implementing a variety of strategies
- Creating continuity in course sequencing and integrating prior learning

III. Motivating Students

- Identifying and addressing study/learning needs
- Identifying and clarifying values
- Discussing motivation theories

IV. Relevance

- Student background
- Practical applications
- Environmental and contextual relevance
- Selection and use of current materials to foster relevancy

This outline became the blueprint for faculty development training, faculty discussions about critical thinking at an open-admissions college, academic and student support programs, resource allocation, and performance evaluations. It represented an effective integration of pragmatic considerations, best practices and research, and the needs of diverse students.

Diversity and Stylistic Differences

I alluded earlier to learning style differences. As I was developing a conceptual model of learning styles, my inclination was to place behaviors in global categories such as Western versus non-Western. This demarcation accounted for the general belief systems and general values associated with how groups perceive them, process information, develop a task orientation, and perceive social interactions (Anderson, 1988, p. 6). For example, I suggested that a

Western orientation to learning places a high emphasis on individual achievement, especially in competitive situations. On the other hand, a non-Western orientation focuses more on the collective effort that promotes achievement and success.

The shortcomings of such a conceptual model are obvious: it does not account for specific factors such as class, culture, race, gender, the nature of classroom dynamics, instructor's expectations, instructional style, prior educational experiences, and parents' educational level. While race and culture can have a powerful effect on students' learning, so, too, can the teaching style of an instructor who is so rigid and inflexible that he or she is not attuned to diverse learning styles.

Schoem, Frankel, Zuniga, and Lewis (1993) suggest that it is important to organize our thinking about multicultural teaching around interconnected dimensions: (a) content, which refers to broadening the curriculum; (b) process and discourse, which refers to different ways of knowing; and (c) diversity of faculty and students, which refers to the representativeness of the backgrounds of those in the classroom. For Butler (1989), who, with others, shaped the curricular transformation efforts at the University of Washington, Seattle, linking of pedagogy and content also acknowledges the presence of the "isms": racism, sexism, classism, and ethnocentrism. This is done not to politicize the curriculum, but to add reality to curricular content and scholarship and to facilitate discourse among students.

Students can develop expectations about instructors based on their preferred learning style. Quite simply, their preference is to have a match between their own style and the instructional style. In previous research (Anderson, 1995, p. 76) I suggested that by using the learning styles associated with field-independence versus field-dependence (sensitivity), we can identify the characteristics associated with this comparison that emphasize how people (students) develop stylistic preferences for certain environmental cues. Persons who use a field-independent style structure information differently in the learning environment from those who are field-sensitive.

Table 4.1 offers one example of the differential expectations of the two groups; Table 4.2 presents a comparison of teaching styles based on a similar comparison.

The research supporting stylistic differences in teaching and learning has primarily been qualitative, survey-based, and correlational, yet it has shown consistency over the last three decades. What has undergone noticeable

TABLE 4.1
What Students Expect From Instructors Based on Preferred Style

Field-Sensitive Orientation	*Field-Independent Orientation*
To give support, show interest, be emotional	To focus on task and objective
To provide guidance modeling and constructive feedback	To provide independence and flexibility
Seek verbal and nonverbal cues to support words	Commands and messages are given directly and articulately
Minimize professional distance	Maximize professional distance
Seek opinions when making decisions and incorporate affective considerations	Make decisions based on analysis of problems and objective criteria
Identify with values and needs of students	Identify with goals and objectives of task

TABLE 4.2
Field-Dependent and Field-Independent Teaching Strategies

Field-Dependent (sensitive)	*Field-Independent*
1. Focuses on needs, feelings, and interests of students	1. Focuses on task
2. Acts as a consultant or supervisor in the classroom	2. Fosters modeling and imitation
3. Uses an informal approach and elicits class discussion	3. Uses a formal, lecture-oriented approach
4. Uses personal rewards	4. Uses impersonal rewards
5. Encourages group achievement	5. Encourages individual achievement
6. Narrates and humanizes concepts	6. Emphasizes facts and principles
7. Identifies with class	7. Remains emotionally detached

change over this period are the topical areas for examination; in other words, there has been more application of study of the topic. For example, in their first book, Sims and Sims (1995) edited a comprehensive compilation of theories, inventories, and real-world examples of learning style application. Their more recent publication (Sims and Sims, 2006) expands those topical areas to include (a) today's increased accountability and testing expectations; (b) learning competencies in a diverse workforce and a global economy; (c) learning effectiveness in noneducational organizations; (d) learning styles and adult learners; (e) learning style assessment and understanding team compositional diversity; and (f) employee training and development. Both longitudinal and experimental research are needed to strengthen the documentation of stylistic differences, their relationship to effective instruction, their interaction with demographic characteristics and sociocultural factors, and their impact on student learning at all educational levels.

Diverse Student Assimilation Versus Adaptation

Colleges and universities are charged—in fact, they have the ethical responsibility to create equitable learning environments in which all students can succeed. Students are expected to enter with basic skills, competencies, and accomplishments and then, over time, to make the necessary adjustments to the culture of college. When diverse students matriculate into institutions, they often experience the dual commitment to college success strategies and to affirming their stylistic preferences. Should they be expected to assimilate, as soon as possible, into what might be a Eurocentric, competitive, and analytical environment?

I see the outcomes associated with assimilation as a significant goal, but I prefer to refer to the process as selective mainstreaming. Assimilation implies that a student is giving up something to take on something else. Selective mainstreaming suggests that you understand the value of making the transition without giving up what you perceive as an asset. It sends the wrong message to a diverse student to suggest that he or she has the necessary credentials to be admitted to the institution, but lacks the cognitive, intellectual, and perceptual assets to be successful. We can make a student feel more valued and empowered when we affirm the important components of his or her assets while also asking the student to expand his or her repertoire of skills and competencies. The teaching and learning environment that encourages and rewards the development of dual assets produces a better student, the classroom becomes a more dynamic environment, and the chances that positive educational outcomes can be realized are enhanced.

Is it the student's responsibility to adapt to the teaching style of the professor, or for the professor to adapt to the learning styles of the students in the classroom? At one of my previous institutions, Indiana University of Pennsylvania, a poll of several hundred professors was conducted during the 1989–90 school year, and the overwhelming response to that question was that students were responsible for adapting to the instructor. During an in-depth interview in the *Forum for Teaching Excellence* at IUP (Zanich, 1990) I disagreed with the faculty's response on several grounds:

1. Most faculty have not learned the dynamics of effective teaching, so their perspective is often limited to what makes them comfortable rather than what helps the student learn. Such faculty's teaching styles tend to be content-centered, not student-centered.

2. Faculty who participate in formal faculty development efforts tend to be more successful in the classroom, have more positive teaching evaluations, and engage learners in more diverse ways. The problem is that on most campuses only a small percentage of faculty actually take advantage of faculty development offerings.

3. Faculty should not make assumptions about student readiness for any mode of teaching. Generally, students are not trained to adapt to varied teaching styles in high school, so why should we assume they can make such a transition in college?

4. The increased diversity of entering students will place more pressure on faculty to respond to their needs. The instructors who remain intransigent are less valued by students, their own colleagues, and the institution.

5. The definition of teaching excellence has expanded to include formal discussions about diversity and its relationship to positive classroom outcomes. Thus, when faculty are reviewed for promotion and tenure, there is greater expectation that they understand that diversity plays a role in the teaching/learning paradigm.

Faculty Attributes and Diversity

The higher education discussion on diversity has typically emphasized the adjustment of underrepresented groups to traditional contexts (classroom and campus climate) and to traditional modes of instruction, and a significant body of work has emerged that sheds light on how to accommodate the needs of diverse learners. Comparing these findings with the opposite scenario is a valuable exercise: instead of relatively homogeneous campuses with predominantly White students and faculty, what if the White faculty were the minority at historically Black colleges and universities (HBCUs)? What factors influence their perception of and adjustment to diversity when they (the faculty) are the underrepresented group?

Smith and Borgstedt (1985) examined the elements, environment, interactions, and/or relationships that directly or indirectly influence the adjustment of White faculty members at an HBCU. Using a Likert-type scale, the researchers sampled 94 participants from four HBCUs in two states and identified 10 attributes that were significant to the faculty:

1. interaction barriers and negative stereotyping (stereotyping);
2. social acceptance and equality in relationships (equality);
3. personal commitment to Black education (commitment);
4. strong racial identity (identity);
5. attitudes of family and friends toward minorities (family and friends);
6. career restrictions (administration);
7. comfort with racial differences (differences);
8. open in dealing with racial differences (openness);
9. conflicts in grading Black students (grading); and
10. feeling trusted by Blacks and being able to trust Blacks (trust)

While most of the attributes are positive (equality, commitment, comfort, and openness, etc.), some can also be viewed as negative (grading conflicts, career restrictions, and stereotyping). What do such opposing distributions suggest? It may be that the dynamics of faculty-student interactions are more complex when White faculty are the racial minority on a campus. An issue such as grading may become more connected to race at an HBCU for White faculty as is the expectation that they also may be more demonstrative in exhibiting racial tolerance and comfort. At a majority campus, students of color spread their expectations across the institution rather than just isolating faculty as a target.

While there were some limitations to the design of the study (the survey instrument needed more items per attribute, and a larger sample size was needed), it is important to note the very introspective nature of faculty perceptions (feelings, perceptions, commitment, acceptance, etc.). Such extensive attention to personal and social attributes has not been reported in the research literature when faculty members address racial diversity on predominant White campuses.

Louis (2005) sought to extend the research of Smith and Borgstedt by identifying additional attributes or expanding on the original 10. For example, he adds more specificity to the original attribute of attitudes of family and friends toward minorities and suggests that more survey items should be developed by each of the following:

- attitude of mother toward minorities;
- attitude of father toward minorities;
- attitude of siblings toward minorities;
- attitude of spouse or partner toward minorities if either the spouse or the partner is White;
- attitude of White colleagues from predominantly White institutions; and
- attitudes of White friends.

Among the new attributes to be examined would be:

- demographics of the community in which participants lived as a child; and
- demographics of the community in which the participants currently live.

An extensive analysis of faculty perceptions and attributes can significantly expand our understanding of climate (classroom and campus) and the factors that underscore the relationship between White faculty and students who are diverse in terms of race or other demographic characteristics. Survey research of this type can be combined with a behavioral analysis of faculty interactions to offer a valid picture of the actual relationship between diversity and instructor-related variables. White faculty who self-assess their own attributes may produce more positive outcomes, such as intellectual development in the classroom, than those faculty who do not.

Do Faculty Interactions Among Diverse Students Enhance Intellectual Development?

A fundamental assumption that underscores the position of those who support incorporating diversity into the dynamics of the college classroom is that positive intellectual and social outcomes will occur. A growing number of studies support this finding (Astin, 1993; Chang, 1999; Goon, 1999); however, most did not use a strong research design. While surveys, focus groups, self-reported data, correlational designs, and ethnographic studies yield important information, what is needed are the results generated by an experimental design. A recent study that appeared in *Psychological Science* not only provides such an experimental framework but also reports results in an extremely valuable area—cognitive development.

Antonio et al. (2004) used a research design that permits examination of the effects of diversity on integrative complexity (IC), which refers to the degree to which students' cognitive style involves differentiation and integration of multiple perspectives. Low IC students take a simple, less complicated approach to reasoning, decision making, and evaluating information. High IC students evaluate, in a reflective way, various perspectives, solutions, and discussion. The researchers used small-group discussions and varied group racial composition and group opinion about a target social issue. Among the significant findings was that the presence of minority students in a group of White students leads to a greater level of cognitive complexity. In addition, the racial diversity of a student's close friends and classmates has a greater impact on IC than does the diversity of the discussion group. This latter finding implies that prolonged contact may have a stronger effect on cognitive complexity than does singular or intermittent contact.

The interaction among diverse student groups within a formal classroom setting forms the basis of mandatory diversity requirements that generally range from 3 to 12 credit hours on many campuses. For example, the University of California, Berkeley has an American cultures (AC) requirement for its undergraduates. Faculty thread comparative analyses of their teaching and research across complex discussions, and the AC requirement is treated as a living, evolving effort that expands in scope as the need arises. Unfortunately, on many campuses, the learning outcomes associated with such requirements are not always evident, nor are they linked to effective teaching strategies.

Concrete Success Strategies and Programs

While many institutions exhibit both symbolic and verbal support for the academic success of diverse student populations, a smaller percentage of colleges and universities have committed to long-term support of concrete programs with proven records of success. Such programs emphasize various aspects of the teaching/learning paradigm and are especially important for science, math, engineering, and technical courses—areas that historically have been problematic for diverse students. The consistency of such programs results from a merger of proven techniques and identification of the students' needs, weaknesses, goals, values, and expectations of diverse populations.

The programs share certain characteristics that establish the framework for the more specific approaches, including:

- They move students from individual levels of academic self-esteem to a sense of collective identity.
- They front-load their activities so that diverse students develop a firm foundation and are better prepared for the more difficult upper-level courses.
- They align entering students with upper-level students, graduate students, and faculty members, in many cases establishing formal mentoring efforts.
- They sustain program excellence by maintaining high standards, rigor, and scholarly nurturing.
- They use a developmental or phase-development process that moves students from lower to higher levels of analytical thinking, problem solving, reasoning, and active learning

The University of Washington has supported a long-running successful program in physics and biology for students of color; Table 4.3 identifies the classroom strategies that are aligned with successful program outcomes.

This program recognizes that even students with good academic profiles can vary significantly in their conceptual and analytical abilities, critical thinking skills, and general level of academic preparation.

To commit to a model of diversity and inclusive teaching, faculty must accept the roles and responsibilities associated with transforming a classroom. The shift from a traditional classroom to one that is transformed is no

TABLE 4.3
Success Strategies for Diverse Students in Courses
With Technical and Abstract Content

1. Exploratory Activity and Questioning
   Prior to formal concept formation and model building students use their own words.

2. Continuous Use of Real-World and Practical Examples

3. Idea First and Name Afterward
   Students are introduced to concepts by examination and observation of objects, situations, and phenomena. Knowledge and understanding come from "shared experience"; they are not just technical terms.

4. Inferences Drawn from Models
   Students should have reasons for what they believe. They should feel free to express success, futility, and wonder in their own words. Early model building should be based on self-initiated activities and direct experience.

5. Use of Analogies
   Students learn to move from relatively simple analogies to ones that are increasingly more complex.

6. Early Identification of Bottlenecks
   "Bottlenecks" represent points in a course where students begin to have conceptual difficulty understanding what's going on. They need to know where they are and what is happening. How does faculty adjust?

7. Laboratory or Experiential Exercises Should Precede or Occur Simultaneously with Lecture

easy task. Many factors can influence such a shift, and they may not all converge at the same time. Table 4.4 compares how characteristics change in the transformative shift.

The move from a traditional to a transformed curriculum connects curricular and pedagogical change. Because such a shift engenders political ambiguity in many, it is important to keep the relationship between diversity and excellence front and center in all discussions.

Unintentional Bias and College Teaching

I consider Craig E. Nelson, a biology professor at Indiana University (Bloomington) to be one of the most active seminal thinkers in higher educa-

TABLE 4.4
Characteristics of the Traditional and Transformed Classroom

Traditional Classroom	*Transformed Classroom*
• Emphasizes traditional canon texts	• Includes nontraditional texts
• Emphasizes limited themes (often Eurocentric) and contexts	• Includes a variety of themes and contexts
• Promotes monocultural perspective	• Encourages alternate perspectives
• Emphasizes instructor as lecturer	• Instructor facilitates collaborative learning
• Deconstructs power of the instructor	• Constructs voice and confidence of the student
• Uses few innovative teaching strategies	• Includes innovative and proven teaching strategies
• Limits classroom to traditional indicators	• Uses a variety of formative and summative classroom assessments

tion. He is a masterful synthesizer who tackles broad and difficult questions and elusive subjects. He has worked extensively with faculty from different disciplines as they examine how bias is unintentionally built into many college classroom practices, and, more important, he offers strategies to make classes fairer without sacrificing learning.

While discussions about bias in the classroom often center on race and gender, Nelson expands his examination to include urban versus rural, college preparatory secondary schools versus traditional secondary schools, issues of class, and the nature of the social system as they all apply to learning. The nature of the questions he frames reflects his comprehensive approach to the dynamics of teaching and learning, and it allows for discussion about the politics of learning while keeping the focus on educational, not political, considerations. This last balancing act is practiced by a few and mastered by even fewer.

On October 2, 1998, Nelson facilitated a retreat for faculty members at North Carolina State University, entitled "Comments and Conversations on Diversity, College Teaching and the Key Role of Inquiry-Guided Instruction." He forced the faculty and administrators in attendance to take an introspective look at the inherent assumptions that underscore their definitions of "effective" instruction and "equity" in the classroom. Examples of the topical questions he used to provoke discourse include:

1. Should I Emphasize Current and Recent Patterns of Discrimination In My Field and In Its Application?
   - Where do different groups fall out of the pipeline to positions of major importance in my field?
   - What is the distribution of student groups in research teams?
   - What is the distribution of groups within and among fields: math, physics, biology?
   - Is there prima facie evidence of discrimination?
2. Should I Make Deep Changes in Classroom Dynamics?
   - Should I adapt a metaphor of teaching more in line with theories of learning as construction versus copying?
   - Should I be visible as a person with an explicit intellectual history, current intellectual commitments and doubts, and explicit value stances?
   - Should I incorporate student experience and dialogue, for example, student-student discussion?
   - Should I foster less competition and more collaboration?
3. To What Extent Does My Grading Scheme Foster Mastery of My Field, and to What Extent Does It Sort Students on Social Class-Based Entry Characteristics?
   - Are there class-based differences in the extent to which students have been trained in the conventions of our discipline?
   - Are there substantial differences in student preparation for long-term time management tasks and in the extent to which their lives are likely to be inflexible (from, e.g., the demands of extensive employment) and seriously interrupted (from, e.g., family problems)? Does fixed-deadline grading tend to exacerbate the impact of the differences?
   - Should I train students to take exams and write papers (in concert with the conventions of the discipline)?
   - Should I use an evaluation system that encourages mastery of the discipline?

At the core of Nelson's beliefs and values about teaching and learning is the preconception that traditionally taught courses incorporate neutral teaching practices. Not only does this severely limit student learning in general, but it also (unintentionally or intentionally) promotes a deep bias in ways that make substantial difference in performance for many students (Nelson, 1996). If uniform high performance across groups is specified as a formal goal, Nelson suggests that emphasis be placed on structured student-student group work. While other authors have researched the value and importance of collaborative learning, only a few have developed a theoretical and practical model that accounts for social class, race, gender, and ethnicity.

It is not the formation and activity of structured groups that produce the greatest benefits; instead, it is the effective discussion that evolves under these three conditions:

- The instructor makes sure the students are prepared for the discussion.
- The students participate in the discussion constructively and fairly evenly.
- The students address questions that are sufficiently challenging and that promote active learning.

Most of the successful undergraduate programs in math, science, and engineering that target the successes of diverse groups use a similar group-based discourse. Among such programs are the Biology Scholars Program at UC, Berkeley; the Meyerhoff Scholars Program at the University of Maryland, Baltimore County; the Science, Technology and Research Scholars (STARS) program at Yale University; the Minority Engineering Program at the University of Michigan; the Carnegie Mellon Action Project (Carnegie Mellon University); the Emerging Scholars Program at the University of Texas at Austin; the Stress On Analytical Reasoning (SOAR) program at Xavier University in New Orleans; and the Physics and Biology Program at the University of Washington.

A similar group of successful programs that emphasize varying levels of mathematics achievements for racially diverse students includes the Mathematics Workshop Program at UC, Berkeley; the Emerging Scholars Programs at the University of Texas; Rutgers University's EXCEL program; and a second Emerging Scholars Program at California Polytechnic State University at San Luis Obispo.

While it is encouraging to know that such programs exist, it is disheartening to recognize that most institutions do not make similar efforts. I have long contended that the issue is not that institutions don't know how to promote excellence among diverse learners, rather, many have lacked the vision and/or abdicated the responsibility. They have the best research, models, and practices at their disposal, yet the institution does not value teaching and learning as the highest priorities. Such a statement is not an indictment of senior leadership or faculty involvement, but on those campuses where multiple indicators of student attrition, disengagement, and learning deficiencies exist, there must be some explanation when attention and resources are not forthcoming to invest in a successful model.

Learning Communities as Authentic Spaces for Intellectual Diversity

Five of the most rewarding years of my professional career were spent as a National Learning Communities Fellow—a designation awarded to approximately 50 colleagues from different two- and four-year institutions who participated in a program housed at Evergreen State College in Olympia, Washington. We had the opportunity to shape the national conversation on the educational reform associated with the development of effective learning communities, especially formulation and documentation of the best research, best practices, and best models.

The successful programs highlighted above share several common characteristics:

- They are in environments that promote a community of engagement among learners and indirectly among faculty.
- Learning becomes a social process rather than an individual one because students learn from one another.
- The programs are flexible enough to accommodate a variety of structured learning processes, including inquiry-guided learning, collaborative learning, problem-based learning, and critical thinking, among other.
- The programs promote equitable curricular and cocurricular activities for diverse learners.
- Linkages can be established across courses and disciplines.
- As students develop skills and competencies, they also learn to value the personal and social attributes that require students to become effective citizens in the 21st century.

- The programs are well conceived and structured, so they submit easily to program assessment and outcomes-based assessment.
- The programs are intellectually rigorous and promote inclusive outcomes.
- Students become comfortable with the complex nature of critical discourse and reflective, inquiry-based thinking.
- Students begin to develop new perspectives on reality, especially the importance of understanding shared realities.

Learning communities provide a safe space where people do not make hurtful judgments about others' characteristics, competencies, values, or politics. While the acceptance of diversity as a shared value by all members of the learning community may take some time, the process of engagement encourages and rewards incremental gains and successes. Even setbacks or missteps are analyzed in the context of being teachable moments. Insertion of diversity and globalism into the teaching and learning paradigm requires the presence of a strong structural undergirding, and learning communities can serve as a powerful construction site that permits, over time, intellectual, personal, and social scaffolding.

References

Anderson, J. A. (1988). Cognitive styles and multicultural populations. *Journal of Teacher Education, 39*, 2–9.

Anderson, J. A. (1995). Toward a framework for matching teaching and learning styles for diverse populations. In R. Sims & S. Sims (Eds.), *The importance of learning styles* (pp. 69–78). Westport, CT: Greenwood Press.

Antonio, A. L., Chang, M. J., Hakuta, K., Denny, D. A., Levin, S., & Milem, J. F. (2004). Effects of racial diversity on complex thinking in college students. *Psychological Science, 15*(8), 507–510.

Astin, A. W. (1993). *What matters in college.* San Francisco: Jossey-Bass.

Ayers-Nachamkin, B. (1992). A feminist approach to the introductory statistics course. *Women's Studies Quarterly, 1 & 2*, 86–94.

Belenky, M. F., Clinchy, B. M., Goldberger, N. R., & Torule, J. M. (1986). *Women's ways of knowing.* New York: Basic Books.

Butler, J. (1989). Transforming the curriculum: Teaching about women of color. In J. Bunks & C. A. Bunks (Eds.), *Multicultural education* (pp. 145–163). Boston: Allyn & Bacon.

Carter, R. T. (1995). *The influence of race and racial identity in psychotherapy: Toward a racially inclusive model.* New York: Wiley.

Chang, M. J. (1999). Does racial diversity matter? The educational impact of a racially diverse undergraduate population. *Journal of College Student Development, 40,* 377–395.

Clinchy, B. M., Belenky, M. F., Goldberger, N., & Torule, J. M. (1985). Connected education for women. *Journal of Education, 167,* 28–45.

Eccles, J. S. & Jacobs, J. E. (1987). Social forces shape math attitudes and performance. In M. R. Walsh (Ed.), *The psychology of women: Ongoing debate* (pp. 341–354). New Haven, CT: Yale University Press.

Goon, P. (1999). The compelling need for diversity in higher education: Expert testimony in *Gratz et al. v. Bollinger et al. Michigan Journal of Race & Law, 5,* 363–425.

Ignelzi, M. (2000, Summer). Meaning-making in the learning and teaching process. *New Directions for Teaching and Learning, 82,* 5–14.

Kegan, R. (1982). *The evolving self: Problem and process in human development.* Cambridge, MA: Harvard University Press.

Lampkin, M. D. (2004). Achieving the dream; First look at the facts. *Change, 36*(6), 12–15.

Louis, D. A. R. (2005). *Attributes influencing the adjustment of White faculty at selected historically black colleges and universities in Texas.* Unpublished doctoral dissertation, Texas A&M University, College Station.

Magolda, M. B. B. (2000). Teaching to promote intellectual and personal maturity: Incorporating students' worldviews and identities into the learning process. *New Directions for Teaching and Learning, 82.*

Musil, C. M. (2001). *Gender, science, and the undergraduate curriculum.* Washington, DC: Association of American Colleges and Universities.

Nelson, C. (1996). Student diversity requires different approaches to college teaching, even in math and science. *American Behavioral Scientist, 40*(2), 165–175.

Ortiz, A. M. (2000). Expressing cultural identity in the learning community: Opportunities and challenges. *New Directions for Teaching and Learning, 82,* 67–79.

Perry, W. G., Jr. (1970). *Forms of intellectual and ethical development in the college years: A scheme.* Austin, TX: Holt, Rinehart and Winston.

Ponterotto, J. G., Casas, J. M., Suzuki, L. A., & Alexander, C. M. (1995). *Handbook of multicultural counseling.* Thousand Oaks, CA: Sage.

Schoem, D., Frankel, L., Zuniga, X., & Lewis, E. A. (1993). *The meaning of multicultural teaching: An introduction.* Westport, CT: Praeger.

Sims, R., & Sims, S. (Eds.). (1995). *The importance of learning styles.* Westport, CT: Greenwood Press.

Sims, R. R., & Sims, S. J. (2006). *Learning styles and learning. A key to meeting the accountability demands in education.* New York: Nova Science Publishers.

Smith, S. L., & Borgstedt, K. W. (1985). Attributes influencing adjustment of White faculty in predominantly Black colleges. *Journal of Negro Education, 54,* 148–163.

Sternberg, R. J. (2005). Accomplishing the goals of affirmative action—With or without affirmative action. *Change, 37*(1), 6–13.

Webb, S. L. (1995). Female-friendly environmental science-building connections and life skills. In S. Rosser (Ed.), *Teaching the majority* (pp. 193–210). New York: Teachers College.

Zanich, M. L. (1990). *In depth: With James Anderson.* Indiana, PA: The Forum for Teaching Excellence, IUP Center for Teaching Excellence.

5

PRACTICAL TEACHING
STRATEGIES THAT ENGAGE
STUDENT DIFFERENCES

Teaching for diversity, that is, teaching to accomplish varied diversity-related outcomes, can be viewed in any number of ways —complicated, political, biased, empowering, prescriptive, non-scholarly, pedagogically necessary, non-Western, inclusive, and empathic. However the process is viewed, the last two decades have witnessed a public confrontation over reshaping the teaching-learning discourse: proponents of equity and diversity in the college classroom have requested a reexamination of the assumptions that underscore traditional academic cultures. Adams (1992) expertly outlines the constrictive nature of traditional classrooms for those populations that reflect different cultures, values, ways of knowing, preferences for learning, identities, social class backgrounds, etc. She appropriately notes that what is critical is "the flexibility of a college instructor's teaching repertoire and his or her readiness to draw on a range of teaching styles for a variety of ends" (p. 15). Teaching for diversity describes an environment of equality in which teaching and learning accentuate the strengths of the instructor and the student, and not only account for differences but use them as an asset in the learning process.

As faculty search for strategies that can expand their repertoire, they should seek frameworks that allow them to remain true to what they value in the discipline *and* provide an effective teaching model for all students. They should affirm all aspects of active and engaged learning as well. Adams and Anderson (1992) use student learning styles as an example of critical considerations with implications for instructional design.

In an earlier chapter I discussed the general difference between content-centered versus student-centered instruction with an emphasis on the perceived role of the instructor in the classroom. Again, student-centered instruction accounts for the diverse needs of all learners and the unique needs of specific populations. Student-centered instruction also appears to be critical to the success of many students of color and other underrepresented groups, especially in those college courses where the abstract course content demands that students exhibit a certain level of analytical skills. While abstract course content is generally associated with gateway courses in math, science, engineering, computer science, accounting, economics, etc., other courses can assume equal difficulty for students when the mode of instruction and the nature of the text (or other written materials) reinforce the abstract and analytical aspects of the information to be learned (philosophy, psychology, etc.).

I must interject two important and connected points here: (a) there should be fewer evaluative judgments about particular approaches to instruction in the college classroom because instructional approaches are neither good or bad, nor are they right or wrong, and (b) the most effective instructional strategies generally are those that are appropriate for particular types of learners under optimal learning conditions. Certain learners prefer content-centered instruction and thrive under such conditions; others do not. Institutions can begin to shape their general and specific expectations for students about the demands and rigors of the culture of college. Using course outcomes, course sequencing, pedagogy, and cocurricular experiences, students can be guided intentionally to use the appropriate learning styles and strategies.

The Implementation of Alternative Pedagogies

At its most fundamental level, pedagogy refers to the way instructors choose to teach and the source(s) of information that influences their decisions about instruction. For those who consciously invest in a commitment to effective teaching, the desire is to link theory to practice and to evaluate specific techniques in terms of the desired course goals and outcomes. Alternative pedagogies, which have evolved as attempts to rethink traditional ways of teaching, represent our best chance to address the challenges and opportunities associated with the increasing diversity among students in the college classroom.

Alternative pedagogies can range from small to moderate improvements of existing, effective teaching strategies to more radical deviations that incorporate sociopolitical considerations. For example, in a discussion about including feminist pedagogy in the teaching of chemistry, Middlecamp and Subramaniam (1999) indicate that as an alternative pedagogy, it (a) describes teaching practices that can benefit all students; (b) offers a way to make science classrooms more inclusive; and (c) provides a framework to examine current teaching practices (p. 520). Such benefits seem reasonable and practical in most discussions about improving college teaching; however, the authors also subscribe to themes that are common to feminist pedagogies: a focus on women, gender, authority, position, empowerment, voice, and non-neutrality. The authors stress the importance of understanding the imbalance of power that is reflected in course content, classroom dynamics, and the goals associated with teaching and learning outcomes. The end result will be to develop pedagogical techniques that benefit all learners, especially those from underrepresented categories.

Webb (1995) suggests that science courses must be transformed to attract and retain women in the science pipeline. She posits several interrelated strategies that become modes of engagement:

1. Urge students to make connections: to real-world problems, across the disciplines, with the instructor as a mentor and role model, and with professionals in the field of science.
2. Use an inclusive pedagogy that does not discourage the "second tier"—those students who are not already committed to science.
3. Promote consistent use of inclusive language that does not distance underrepresented groups from science or the classroom milieu.
4. Explore the human face of scientific controversies, especially when it conflicts with the perceived objectivity of science.
5. Foster cumulative development of scientific and life skills as explicit components of the course content.

The proponents of alternative pedagogies tend to be faculty who find a common thread throughout teaching, scholarship, and service. Stanley et al. (2003) found this to be the case among African American faculty at predominately White research universities. In their case, multicultural teaching complemented their faculty work as a whole.

Alternative Pedagogies: A Chemistry Example

Dr. Rabi Musah, an associate professor of chemistry at the University at Albany, is passionate about at least two things: increasing students' success rate in undergraduate chemistry courses and motivating young females to think about chemistry as a career. Her efforts translate into working with minority high school female students to engage them in projects that are relevant, real-world, and promote genuine learning outcomes. In one example, her students analyze the impact that certain chemical dyes have on food and drink, especially as they might contribute to health disparities in women, minorities, and the poor. Rather than teach the abstractions of chemical concepts in a traditional pedagogical context, she immerses these students into exciting research that involves social and political considerations and solidifies learning in both the cognitive and affective domains.

In an attempt to use an alternative pedagogy in teaching college chemistry courses, Musah and her colleagues have developed the interdisciplinary Undergraduate Research Collaborative Project, whose goals are to (a) enhance academic performance in a chemistry course; (b) to increase student involvement in undergraduate research; (c) increase the number of diverse students who engage in both chemistry and undergraduate research; and (d) present chemistry to the students in a real-world context. One project capitalizes on the national interest students are exhibiting in forensic analysis. Students are required to perform a mineral analysis of soil samples that could be drawn from the shoes or clothing of individuals who allegedly have engaged in criminal activity. The database the students produce is mapped relative to geoquadrants in and around the city, which, in turn, will be linked to a global positioning satellite.

Student groups that reflect particular interests can form within such projects. A cadre of female students might target alleged perpetrators involved in crimes against women and children; another group might examine soil samples extracted from automobile tires in high-traffic drug markets. Alternative pedagogies allow for, in fact encourage, the academic pursuit of topics and considerations that also reward the affective dimension of learners.

Program Success and Instructional Type

One approach to examining varied modes of instruction and how different student populations respond to them is to identify the characteristics of effective instruction in highly successful programs for diverse students. For example, certain programs are able to move students from one identified level of cognitive development to another. They also may promote active learning and student responsibility for learning. In such programs participants may not appear at the start of the course to be as academically competitive as students with higher entering academic profiles, yet they often equal or surpass this latter group in terms of actual performance. Finally, such programs are consistent, that is, they exhibit longitudinal success and are underscored by models that reflect best practices and high standards of performance.

Table 5.1 lists some of the characteristics of effective instruction that Anderson (1994, p. 99) has reported earlier in his examination of successful programs for diverse students across disciplines at two- and four-year institutions.

TABLE 5.1
Characteristics of Effective Instructions for Students Who Are Diverse by Demographic Category and Skill Level

The Instructor:

1. Fosters a sense of community among students that is grounded on the shared experience of doing serious work.
2. Identifies and acknowledges the developmental skill level of students and gears instruction and course materials to that level.
3. Individualizes and personalizes classroom presentations when necessary, while maintaining student focus on a standard of excellence.
4. Encourages students to express their reasoning processes in their own words, especially when they struggle with abstract course content.
5. Uses students' feedback periodically to assess student progress and the impact of instruction.
6. Engages the students with structured and collaborative tasks, hands-on activities, and incremental challenges.
7. Guides students in learning how to frame new questions that allow them to explore deeper levels of learning.
8. Guides students in the use of alternate learning strategies.
9. Introduces information to be learned in a manner that correlates with what is relevant and familiar to students.
10. Requires students to make connections among isolated pieces of information.
11. Provides appropriate feedback to students' questions, errors, and conceptual difficulties.
12. Varies instructional methods according to expected learning outcomes.

Effective instructional approaches do not occur in a vacuum; instead, they are complemented by student behaviors and learning outcomes. The aforementioned techniques become more effective as students incorporate successful learning strategies into their classroom activities. Diverse students can acquire the strategies at their own developmental pace, but the gains tend to occur more frequently within some type of systematic collaborative learning framework.

Table 5.2 identifies examples of strategies that are appropriate for courses that cause bottlenecks for students because of the analytical or abstract nature of their content. A bottleneck can be thought of as any point in a course when students begin to exhibit conceptual difficulty understanding the content. Overcoming early bottlenecks is often a prerequisite to negotiating those that occur later.

TABLE 5.2
Successful Learning Strategies Exhibited by Diverse Students in Courses With Abstract and Technical Content

The Student:
1. Engages in exploratory activity and questioning. Before formal concept formation and model building, students use their own words and examples to discuss the information to be learned.
2. Prefers to address abstract concepts by examining and observing objects, situations, and phenomena. Students also draw from their shared experiences with other students.
3. Attempts to draw inferences from models. Early model building should be based on self-initiated activities and direct experience. As students draw inferences from models, they offer reasons for what they believe. They feel confident in expressing success, confusion, and wonder in their own words.
4. Learns to move from relatively simple analogies to those that are increasingly more complex. Understands that analogical thinking is a more demanding learning strategy that separates preformal thinkers from formal thinkers.
5. Begins to practice and value meta-cognitive tools. Assertively identifies and attacks conceptual "bottlenecks"—points in a course where students begin to have conceptual difficulty understanding what's going on. Students desire to know why such difficulties are happening and how they should be addressed. Students also systematically examine the errors they make.
6. Uses real-world and practical examples to move upward to a more refined level of concept formation, reasoning, and critical thinking.
7. Recognizes the need to transition between one set of learning styles/strategies and another set when information suggests it.

One way instructors can enhance the attractiveness of abstract course content for a broader range of learners is to build classroom instructional techniques around specific outcomes that encourage students to become more fluent as they learn the discipline. For example, traditional mathematics outcomes involve some level of conceptual understanding and problem solving, and students usually are expected to demonstrate such competencies on tests or in homework assignments. The addition of two other outcomes can also facilitate student confidence:

- Students will develop mathematical reasoning skills by applying examples that reflect real-world situations, especially those that are relevant and familiar to them.
- Students will learn to put mathematical language into everyday language and practice oral presentations to a variety of audiences.

In terms of instructional strategies, the first outcome requires the instructor to have a student-centered understanding of the incentives and situations that enhance student attention, motivation, and task completion. The second outcome may require instructors to participate in faculty development workshops that emphasize writing and speaking in the disciplines. An excellent example of using both outcomes involves ethnomathematics, which links students' diverse ways of knowing and learning and culturally embedded knowledge with academic mathematics. It attempts to demystify the belief that certain racial, ethnic, and/or gender groups do not have the innate ability to comprehend complex mathematics. Powell and Frankenstein (1997) challenge the Eurocentric assumptions in mathematics education by asking students to examine the connection between math and the power relationship in our various organizational systems. Students examine contemporary issues in the media—issues that are often relevant to them—and assess the kind of mathematical knowledge necessary to understand and evaluate each issue (Duranczyk et al., 2004, p. 47).

Diversity Outcomes and Learning Paradigms

As instructors consider applying various pedagogies that facilitate implementation of diversity outcomes, attention should be given to models of learning that historically have benefited a diverse range of learners, that engage students cognitively and affectively, and that allow students to translate their academic training into real-world problem solving. Two modes of learning that represent such fertile environments are cooperative learning and service learning. Both approaches represent structured opportunities that engage students in dynamic learning environments that, in turn, can produce practical outcomes.

In an attempt to blur the boundaries between college and the community, LaGuardia Community College in New York requires all students to engage in a cooperative learning experience that (a) connects them to the community; (b) allows them to learn how systems function; (c) expects them to be active participants ("to be in the room and at the table"); and (d) asks them to think critically and reflectively about their experience. Faculty support the cooperative engagement through supervision, monitoring, encouragement, and evaluation. The following three examples reflect practical and diversity-related outcomes:

- Students attempted to help international members of the community acquire their citizenship. To do so they had to learn about the immigration system and establish trust with community members, in this case Koreans. During this project the students learned that Korean drycleaners were out of compliance with the new Environmental Protection Agency (EPA) guidelines and requirements, which could lead to huge monetary fines. Student diligence and commitment contributed to educating the store owners who were brought into compliance while increasing the number of successful applications for citizenship.
- LaGuardia Community College wanted to engage the allied health program students in their respective communities to understand and experience the real world of public health. The students worked on a project that examined the link between asthma and socioeconomic status. Although they initially went into the community as student researchers, they ultimately returned home as applied practitioners.
- As is often the case in large metropolitan urban areas, what was once private community property can become subsumed by practical needs. In this case, a cemetery in the Black community was being converted into a parking lot. Students took on a project researching layers of history that were associated with the community. Such documentation represents a palpable legacy that might have been lost forever.

All of these examples represent an approach that is consistent with the recent changes in education that shift from a focus on teaching to a focus on student learning and engagement. Moreover, students interacted with diverse communities, and they developed a deeper understanding of the subject.

Service Learning as a Paradigm for Engagement

Service learning is a form of experiential education in which students engage in activities that address human and community needs, together with structured opportunities intentionally designed to promote student learning and development, reflection, and reciprocity (Duffy, 2000). When applied to any discipline, service learning requires students to consider communities' social and cultural context, to develop the ability to ask serious questions about their own involvement, and to evaluate information objectively. In disciplines where new curriculum guidelines call for including social and ethical implications (by regional and national accreditors), service learning represents a valuable pedagogical fit as long as the pedagogical and instructional models align with the expected learning outcomes. Activities that produce some external social or political impact but little learning do not meet the true criteria associated with a service-learning activity.

Service Learning and the Inclusion of Culture

Despite the rhetoric that often presents community-campus partnerships as mutually beneficial to one another, it is important to frame such relationships in terms of the cultural framework in which they occur. Service learning represents a pedagogy of engagement comprised of inputs, processes, methods, and outcomes and the interrelationship among these variables can create complexity (Lowery et al., 2006, p. 48). A recognition and understanding of diversity and culture as they apply to service learning can help the partners to (a) be aware of individual and collective beliefs; (b) align their expectations with reality; and (c) positively influence outcomes by intentionally using language that is familiar to all partners (Kecskes, 2006, p. 7). For example, service learning that is guided by a hierarchical framework tends to be transactional or instrumental—parties engage because each has something the other needs to complete a task. However, no long-term change is expected, and neither partner alters the framework very much. In many cases, this framework allows campuses to help a needy community while allowing students to put theory into practice. Colleges and universities must resist the temptation to believe they have all of the assets and expertise to meet a community's needs.

More beneficial to the community-campus partnership is a framework that promotes dialogue, mutual responsibility, group decision making, and consensus. Service learning that reflects equal participation is based on an egalitarian orientation and respects the views, attitudes, and expectations of culture groups within the community. This framework enhances the expected learning outcomes associated with reflection, since learning can be placed in a cognitive and affective context.

For example, one computer technology requirement is social impact analysis (SIA)—a process that allows student teams to gain experience in assessing the impact of a particular computer system in a real-world setting with real stakeholders. Martin (2000) cited examples in which student teams conducted SIA at various community agencies (senior service centers, care centers for homeless children, daycare centers, etc.). The teams identified immediately that the equipment was useless and obsolete, but they also saw the paucity of equipment as an equity and access issue that disempowers diverse communities. The result was an enhanced learning experience and students' raised consciousness. In terms of cognitive and reflective outcomes, students move to a higher level of thinking about the application of technology and its relationship to social class, race, and poverty; even more important, their affective and evaluative judgments become increasingly more analytical.

A more provocative example can be seen in applying service learning and diversity to biological and agricultural engineering by Marybeth Lima, an associate professor at Louisiana State University (LSU). Lima uses a pedagogy through which she can cultivate understanding in engineering students of the social and historical aspects of people, culture, and society that are central to the design process and to problem solving. In other words, she articulates both learning outcomes and global competencies.

Biology in Engineering (BE 1252) is a two-credit-hour, second-semester-freshman core course in which students integrate learning experiences with a semester-long service-learning project involving the design of playgrounds in diverse communities such as Baton Rouge, Louisiana. In the course undergraduate students collaborate closely with teachers, students, and administrators at a target elementary school in all aspects of the process, including design, fundraising, and implementation. Classroom activities correspond to steps encountered in the engineering design process, and each student is required to maintain a student portfolio (Christy & Lima, 1998). The elementary school links the course involvement to the K–5 students' science and math education, and, as was the case in the previous example, the learning outcomes of the course—engineering design concepts and process—become more meaningful because of real-world considerations.

This service-learning project offers students the opportunity to link their academic training to a community, to cross racial and economic boundaries, and to experience civic and social responsibility. At a conference, Lima (2000) reported that the project has also resulted in a 93% freshman-to-sophomore retention rate for women and minorities over three years, which is substantially higher than the national average—a significant added value. To date, her students have designed six playgrounds that serve approximately 300 elementary students, and Dr. Lima's goal is to affect a total of 40 playgrounds.

As LSU's first Service-Learning Faculty Fellow, Marybeth Lima epitomizes dedication to her discipline, to pedagogy, to diversity, to student engagement and learning, to community service, and, most important, to making a difference in the world.

Managing Service Learning

Norfolk State University's (NSU) Service-Learning Center represents a centralized hub for department-based projects. The goal of the center, according to NSU's Office of Institutional Effectiveness and Assessment, is to "enable the University to meet identified community needs and provide NSU students with academically based opportunities for civic engagement." Seventeen academic departments and programs generate service learning-infused courses.

The university's Strategic Planning Committee maintains a database, identifies resources and needs, integrates service learning across disciplines, and cultivates collaborative partnerships with external organizations and community partners. Faculty, departments, and programs receive a template of instructional "best practices" that includes:

- curricular goals,
- assessment,
- service goals,
- evaluation,
- challenges,
- support,
- participation,
- diversity,
- community connections,
- participant preparation,
- reflection, and
- celebration.

At the site level of the service-learning project, the following "best practices" are also adhered to:

- mission, beliefs, and goals;
- policy;
- funding;
- transportation;
- scheduling;
- administrative support;
- risk management;
- coordination of practice and resources;
- service-learning training; and
- ongoing professional development.

NSU's service-learning initiative seeks to promote civic engagement and social responsibility, to have faculty and students engage in experiential teaching and learning, to understand course content at deeper levels of reflection, and to develop sustainable collaborations with the external community. As a historically Black institution, NSU expands its involvement in diverse communities through service learning and, simultaneously, develops 21st-century competencies in their students.

Course-Centered Dialogue Groups

Many factors influence the quality and type of intergroup relations that occur in the college classroom. If a course goal is to produce constructive, instructive, and learning-centered interactions, then the instructor must select both the process and structure that will lend to the desired outcomes. Zuniga and Nagda (1993, p. 234) suggest that structured dialogue groups represent an intervention that addresses the challenge of producing positive intergroup interactions, and an innovative approach to multicultural learning. Dialogue groups can be used across disciplines and/or in courses where the emphasis of the course content is some aspect of diversity or multiculturalism.

Although there are some similarities among student group interactions, dialogue groups represent a discussion format that generally involves members of two self-identified social groups. The groups may vary by race, gender, religious affiliation, sexual orientation, or other prominent categories. While acknowledging that students enter dialogue groups with varying expectations, their participation in such groups allows them to analyze their self-perceptions and preconceived ideas and attitudes objectively.

The authors identify four tasks associated with implementing dialogue groups: identifying the intergroup focus, selecting and training dialogue group facilitators, organizing and supervising, and developing educational resources. Each task must be fully developed and completed to assure the expected cumulative impact. As one might expect, the dialogue group process is structured according to a developmental approach to group work (p. 241).

Challenges and Dilemmas

Instructors who incorporate dialogue groups into classroom dynamics must be true to the formal aspects of structure and process. In addition, they must account for and factor in important challenges and dilemmas. Among these are:

- Falling into the trap of confusing dialogue with debate. The former allows for creativity and open communication; the latter emphasizes confrontation and rigid, non-negotiable discourse.
- Reducing students' fear of conflict, thereby encouraging them to explore and learn from each other.
- Challenging students to recognize the reciprocal impact they have on each other's identities and learning.

- Asking students to think about differences at the micro and individual levels of analysis as well as the macro or group level.
- Expecting facilitators to assume a demanding responsibility while functioning as a peer facilitator.
- Maintaining the group identity associated with the primary intergroup focus as other individual and group identities seek to emerge.

Faculty members cannot underestimate the care needed to incorporate dialogue groups into traditional academic course content, and even more attention and rigor must be applied when faculty establish enhanced pedagogical goals in the classroom, such as those with course goals like active learning, those that address contemporary and controversial topics, those that have interdisciplinary goals, and those that seek to interconnect areas such globalism-social responsibility-civic engagement. For many faculty such explorations sit on the periphery of their understanding of traditional classroom teaching.

Donovan and Veroff (1993) deal with several of these concerns in a second-level social psychology course, titled Personal Organization and Social Organization, which addresses a central question: How does the social environment influence the development and adaptation of the individual? The course incorporates two activities that promote student-student collaboration and active learning: designing an empirical study and collecting data to test the study's hypothesis, and leading at least one class discussion with one or two other students. Course readings reflect the realities of diverse groups and force students to ask and answer difficult questions. Students were encouraged to select some aspect of diversity for their research project while understanding that complex issues can best be addressed in open and authentic discourse.

The final product of dialogue groups can be dynamic learning environments where students move from individual to collective identities, listen to each other with an analytical ear, reinforce each other's learning styles, and reduce the tension that often follows discussion of volatile topics. One by-product might be that they transfer their newly acquired skills to other courses and out-of-class interactions with students who are different.

Dialogue groups can also encompass more comprehensive outcomes. The University of Wisconsin-Milwaukee has developed a comprehensive interdisciplinary program to create globally literate students. One component of the program asks students to enroll in four one-credit "Think Tank Learning Communities" courses. Students engage one another in projects related to current global issues and apply new knowledge in analyzing challenging case studies. The program is sequential, has clearly defined learning outcomes, and intersects several disciplines; this last strategy often has the most significant impact on student learning, cognitive development, and critical literacy competencies.

Global Economics and Elementary Education

As suggested earlier, when faculty alter their instructional styles to transform the curriculum and/or promote diversity-related learning outcomes, they should provide opportunities for students to translate classroom-based academic experiences to real-world scenarios that extend beyond the classroom. When this process occurs effectively, everyone benefits: the instructor, the student, and the group or community that benefits from the academic interventions.

In the previous examples, service learning was identified as a formal process that aligns classroom teaching, theory, student reflection, and community partners. A similar but less formal approach can promote comparable, but less potent, outcomes. At many business schools on college and university campuses, students learn to make a difference in their communities and to develop leadership, teamwork, and communication skills through learning, practicing, and teaching the principles of free enterprise. In the following example, the instructor links the theoretical discussion of free enterprise and global economics with an external student project, called "PenciCola," a service-learning exercise that seeks to educate elementary school students about real-world economics and production in terms they can understand.

Students in a college business course identify an elementary school where teachers and administrators allow their students to participate in an educationally valuable project. The younger students undertake the task of figuring out how a simple wooden pencil with an eraser is made. The primary goal associated with this task is to understand a simple global concept—how do 17 countries work together to produce one pencil? This exercise takes on more meaning when the elementary students are asked to think about the economics of globalization in terms of a product that most of them use and all of them are familiar with—Coca-Cola. As part of the project, the school children purchase Coca-Cola products with indigenous currency of various countries, for which they have exchanged American currency. In doing so, this exercise becomes a lesson on how the world cooperates and how boundaries have begun to shrink. The project not only influences the business students' course grades, it can also be submitted to a national competition. This idea is a product of Students in Free Enterprise (SIFE), a nonprofit organization that works in partnership with business and higher education. It was founded in 1975, and is active on more than 1,600 campuses and in 40 countries.

Instructional Integrity and Students with Disabilities

Implicit in the discussion about diversity and educational excellence is the assumption that inclusiveness is fundamental to all groups. Students with disabilities are ensured equal access by law to the resources and benefits available to all other students. Yet, they are often relegated to a select category, while race, ethnicity, gender, and first-generation and socioeconomic status receive more attention in retention studies. Belch (2004, p. 8) suggests that the same complex factors that interfere with retention of first-time college students in general should be applied to disabled students. Moreover, many strategies that facilitate the engagement and persistence of disabled students are equally effective for those without disabilities.

Students with disabilities are those who have a physical or mental impairment that substantially limits one or more of their major life activities. The range of conditions often associated with disabilities can be described legally and diagnostically in a formal sense and can be confused with difficulties not related to the disability. For example, a first-generation college student who exhibits low academic performance, English as a second language, a less analytical learning style, critical literacy deficiencies (oral and written), and a very reserved demeanor might be perceived as having a disability when the reality might simply be a lack of preparation for college. The opposite is also true, that is, some faculty may view and treat students with bona fide learning disabilities as low performing and academically underprepared.

Jane Jarrow (2005), director of disability policy and education for the Council on Education, describes the steps that are necessary to develop and implement universal design and retention components: (a) figure out how the activity/strategy to be used works for students *without* disabilities; (b) think about how students with various disabilities might have difficulty fully participating in what you have planned for everyone else; and (c) think about what must be incorporated to ensure the elements needed for full participation are part of your design.

Disabled college students are protected by two mandates: section 504 of the 1973 Rehabilitation Act and the Americans with Disabilities Act of 1990. Both acts focus on equal opportunity and access, and not on success, which can translate into a lack of on-time academic supports or appropriate classroom instruction. For example, gateway courses refer to those college courses that are often problematic because of difficult course content; they represent initial courses in a sequence of courses in a major or minor; and success in those courses usually requires some combination of effective analytical competencies and information-processing skills. A disabled student may require an accommodation that the professor does not think is necessary, nor is the accommodation available to other students in the course (specialized tutoring versus generic tutoring, extra time on tests, or unique technology challenges).

At a particular community college (New York City) a course on biological and medical lab technology not only requires that students exhibit some level of technology competency, but it also includes timed group work. In one week students are expected to download source material from a Web site, select a group captain, decide on the order of presentation among group members, etc. While this sequence of tasks can be challenging for the average abled student, it requires disabled students to perform to the same standard. Simonelli (2006) describes how she creates several options or tracks for students to select from. In the more experientially oriented track, they can choose a method to demonstrate their new learning (a creative presentation, a graph or map, a verbal report, etc.). Implicit learning is a central focus for this track, hence Simonelli requires an exercise involving written reflection as well (p. 158).

Universal instructional design (UID) refers to an instructional approach that integrates accommodations at the curriculum design stage capable of being accessed by a wide array of students. As a mode of instruction, UID provides students with multiple means of representation (image versus text), multiple means of expression of the level of learning/knowledge, and multiple means of engagement in the learning process. For Belch (2004, p. 13), students with or without disabilities can personalize the learning experience based on their preferred learning style. Visual learners can translate text and speech to visual images online, and verbal learning can generate the opposite conversion. UID does not require instructors to alter course content, so curricular outcomes can be maintained. Instructors are required to emphasize student accessibility to information. It is ironic that UID comes closer to the educational goals of "meeting the diverse needs of all learners" and "attending to the unique needs of selected learners" than do many other traditional pedagogies.

Incorporating universal design strategies requires a high degree of thoughtful innovation primarily because it involves curriculum planning that provides multiple pathways into learning as intrinsic rather than as a special accommodation for particular students (Simonelli, 2006). For example, using Gardner's (1993) theory of Multiple Intelligences, one can design diverse tasks and activities that are meaningful and that make learning come alive. Thus, the key words associated with each of the seven areas of intelligence can be used to guide planning (mathematical/logical, verbal/linguistic, musical, bodily kinesthetic, interpersonal, intrapersonal, and visual/spatial). Using multiple pathways for learning and varied student groupings encourages a differentiation in instruction.

Many faculty misperceive the place of disabled students in the educational equation. The perception is often that they need "extra help," which places an "extra burden" on the instructor. Most vociferous with such complaints are content-centered instructors. They should view the adaptive needs of disabled students in the same context as the needs of any diverse learner or group of learners, and it is the ethical responsibility of faculty to promote equity in the classroom by incorporating the appropriate adaptive technology.

The Scholarship of Teaching for Diversity

Because pedagogy is not widely seen as a legitimate focus for disciplinary scholarship, it is more difficult to make the case to faculty that pedagogy is worthy of their support and of departmental consideration. The politics of diversity in the academy can lead to an even tougher sell to a traditional academic market. I argued earlier that effective application of diverse pedagogies benefits all students, and proven strategies continue to emerge that support this contention. Sometimes, however, the most sustained academic discussions on diversity must still be converted to a vernacular that traditional faculty value and find meaningful.

What is needed is to elevate this discussion to one of intellectual inquiry that complements the disciplines and provides faculty with an infrastructure to develop their academic and professional careers. The discussion about how this should be accomplished could follow two significant initiatives: (a) the arguments presented in the 1990s by Ernest Boyer and his Carnegie Foundation colleagues who argue for greater recognition and rewards for a wider range of scholarly activity (Boyer, 1990), and (b) the evolution of the work of the Carnegie Academy for the Scholarship of Teaching and Learning (CASTL, 1999).

Drawing on the conclusions from both important initiatives, the direction is clear, and teaching for diversity must be viewed as:

- something that is embraced by the community of scholars, not just by the supporters of diversity;
- a process that strengthens intellectual communities and advances teaching in a scholarly way;
- an artifact that facilitates the reconnection of teaching to the discipline but also expands the purpose and meaning of both to wider audiences in the academy; and
- a product of excellence that is amenable to peer judgment, scholarly examination, and replication of significant results.

Such an approach builds and documents the case for the relationship between educational excellence and diversity, and it opens the door of involvement to those faculty whose previous hesitance about supporting diversity reflected a dissonance associated with the normative expectations and demands of their curriculum and academic department. In a recent conversation with my colleagues at the University at Albany, a group of faculty were asked to participate in a Ford Foundation-funded Difficult Dialogues Project. Younger faculty exhibited a heightened interest at the prospect of such participation leading to more academic publications, potential new research agendas, and avenues for external funding—all of which enhance their opportunities for future promotion and tenure. In an earlier chapter, I emphasized the importance of presenting diversity initiatives as incentives to regular faculty work and faculty value systems. For some this represents a daunting task fraught with political potholes, but others can consider it to be the overlooked catalyst that excites faculty to consider new levels of excellence.

While there might be consensus on how to conceptualize diversity as a scholarly activity, it will be the faculty at individual institutions who will further shape that meaning to reflect things such as institutional type, mission and vision, and the perceived role of the faculty in defining excellence. For example, I conducted a faculty workshop in May 2006 at the College of Mount Saint Joseph in Cincinnati, Ohio. In a discussion on diversity and curricular transformation, I asked the faculty to characterize their perceptions of a compelling case for diversifying the curriculum. They identified the following:

- The learner finds intrinsic interest in the topic when it has been diversified or transformed.
- The learner is able to express divergent perspectives after participating in engaged activities associated with varied readings.
- An inclusive curriculum incorporates topics that are current, relevant, and motivate students to sustain engagement of the topic.
- The content encourages students to engage in a broad debate while using multiple frames of reference (theory, research, problem-based applications, literature, religion, etc.).

Several factors underscored the participants' responses: the liberal arts tradition, the college's mission as a Catholic institution, the desire to connect to the core curriculum outcomes associated with globalism, a respect for the importance of inquiry and reflection, and an awareness of the demographic and conceptual homogeneity of the college's student population. It would behoove any campus to make a public statement about the compelling motivation behind the desire to align traditional content in many disciplines with a broader, more nontraditional body of work. Not to do this is to suggest, tacitly or overtly, that an inclusive curriculum must be introduced furtively—as if we are trying to sneak 21st-century preparation and outcomes into the undergraduate and graduate experiences of students.

References

Adams, M. (1992). Cultural inclusion in the American college classroom. *New Directions for Teaching and Learning, 49,* 5–17.

Adams, M., & Anderson, J. A. (1992). Acknowledging the learning styles of diverse student populations: Implications for instructional design. *New Directions for Teaching and Learning, 49,* 19–33.

Anderson, J. A. (1994). Examining teaching styles and student learning styles in science and math classrooms. In M. M. Atwater (Ed.), *Multicultural education: Inclusion of all* (pp. 93–106). Athens: University of Georgia Press.

Belch, H. A. (2004). Retention and students with disabilities. *Journal of College Student Retention, 6*(1), 3–22.

Boyer, E. C. (1990). *Scholarship reconsidered: Priorities of the professoriate.* Princeton, NJ: Carnegie Foundation for the Advancement of Teaching.

CASTL. (1999). *Information and applications for the Pew National Fellowship Program for Carnegie Scholars.* Menlo Park, CA: Carnegie Foundation for the Advancement of Teaching.

Christy, A., & Lima, M. (1998). Student portfolios in engineering instruction. *Journal of Engineering Education, 87*(2), 143–148.

Donovan, E., & J. Veroff. (1993). Social psychology. In D. Schoem, L. Frankel, X. Zuniga, & E. A. Lewis (Eds.), *Multicultural teaching in the university* (pp. 218–230). Westport, CT: Praeger Press.

Duffy, J. (2000). Service-learning in a variety of engineering courses. In E. Tsang (Ed.), *Projects that matter: Concepts and models for service-learning in engineering* (pp. 75–98). Sterling, VA: Stylus (originally published by American Association for Higher Education).

Duranczyk, I., Staats, S., Moore, R., Hatch, J., Jensen, M., & Somdahl, C. (2004). Introductory-level college mathematics explored through a sociocultural lens. In I. Duronczyk et al. (Eds.), *Best practices for access and retention in higher education* (pp. 43–54). Minneapolis: Center for Research on Developmental Education and Urban Literacy, University of Minnesota.

Gardner, H. (1993). *Multiple intelligences: The theory in practice.* New York: Harper Collins Publishers, Inc.

Jarrow, J. (2005). *Understanding the law: ADA and higher education.* Workshop presentation, Council on Education National Conference, Los Angeles, CA.

Kecskes, K. (2006). Behind the rhetoric: Applying a cultural theory lens to community-campus partnership development. *Michigan Journal of Community Service Learning, 12*(2), 5–14.

Lima, M. (2000). Service-learning: A unique perspective on engineering education. In E. Tsang (Ed.), *Projects that matter: Concepts and models for service-learning in engineering* (pp. 109–118). Sterling, VA: Stylus (originally published by American Association for Higher Education).

Lowery, D., May, D. L., Duchane, K. A., Coulter-Kern, R., De'Bryant, M. P.V., Pomery, J. G., & Bellner, M. (2006). A logic model of service-learning: Tensions and issues for further consideration. *Michigan Journal of Community Service Learning, 12*(2), 47–60.

Martin, C. D. (2000). Integrating service-learning into computer science through a social impact analysis. In E. Tsang (Ed.), *Projects that matter: Concepts and models for service-learning in engineering* (pp. 99–107). Sterling, VA: Stylus (originally published by American Association for Higher Education).

Middlecamp, C. H., & Subramaniam, B. (1999). What is feminist pedagogy? Useful ideas for teaching chemistry. *Journal of Chemical Education, 76*(4), 520–525.

Powell, A. C., & Frankenstein, M. (1997). Ethnomathematical praxis in the curriculum. In A. B. Powell and M. Frankenstein (Eds.), *Ethnomathematics: Challenging Eurocentrism in mathematics education* (pp. 249–260), Albany, NY: State University of New York Press.

Simonelli, S. (2006). Embracing diverse learning styles: Inviting the whole self into learning through the arts, emotion, the body, and direct experience. In R. Sims & S. Sims (Eds.), *Learning styles and learning: A key to meeting the accountability demands in education* (pp. 143–161). New York: Nova Science Publishers.

Stanley, C. A., Porter, M. E., Simpson, N. J., & Ouellett, M. L. (2003). A case study of the teaching experiences of African American faculty at two predominately White research universities. *Journal on Excellence in College Teaching, 14*(1), 151–178.

Webb, S. L. (1995). Female-friendly environmental science: Building connections and life skills. In S. Rossor (Ed.), *Teaching the majority* (pp. 193–210). New York: Teachers College Press.

Zuniga, X., & Nagda, B. (1993). Dialogue groups: An innovative approach to multicultural learning. In D. Schoem, L. Frankel, X. Zuniga, & E. A. Lewis (Eds.), *Multicultural teaching in the university* (pp. 233–248). Westport, CT: Praeger Press.

6

BALANCING THE TRADITIONAL CURRICULUM WITH INCLUSION AND DIVERSITY

I t is often the case on many college campuses that new initiatives either evolve or remain stagnant relative to the degree of institutional readiness—structural, political, procedural, temporal, etc. Even when an initiative has the opportunity to be launched its short-term or long-term prospects are affected by the presence of multiple factors that are associated with readiness.

Curricular change, whether traditional or transformative, is always embedded in an institutional framework. Thus, those leading transformative change must be attuned to cues that suggest a unified set of goals can be embraced, that a commitment to work for change can assume an intrinsic value, and that the courage to face significant barriers has reached a threshold of sustainability.

As campuses frame the questions for discussion, the level of readiness will dictate the type of discourse. A campus that generally is hesitant about change would need to start by considering some seminal questions, such as:

- At our institution, what does it mean to diversify the curriculum?
- What is the impact of an inclusive curriculum on undergraduate education? What will the specific benefits be to students and to the faculty?
- Can we use the existing processes and structures to transform the curriculum or do we need new/modified ones?
- What are the barriers hampering our ability to produce a transformed curriculum?

- Will diversity and globalism be considered as part of our transformation efforts?

On the other hand, a campus at a more advanced stage of readiness may have already adopted a systematic planning process and reviewed previous diversity projects to better inform leaders about future directions. Discussions on curricular change may focus more on process as opposed to knowledge acquisition.

Questions at this level might include:

- What project activities might accompany curricular change? How should they be implemented?
- What resources are needed to initiate and sustain faculty involvement?
- What is the best size and composition of teams when cooperative learning is selected as the classroom dynamic to accompany curricular inclusion?
- Who will develop and manage the assessment plan to determine whether curricular transformation produced the expected impact?
- What are the key questions that will guide faculty development efforts, particularly as faculty redesign the departmental curriculum?
- How do varied definitions of diversity affect students' perceptions of classroom climate? Are such perceptions different for different types of courses?

The following summary serves as an example of how the last question was addressed at North Carolina State University in the 2001–2002 school year. Dr. Marilee Bresciani led a team conducting survey research to identify students' perceptions of classroom climate. Before responding to 38 statements that represented the gist of the survey, student respondents were asked to define diversity relative to 13 dichotomous bio- and sociodemographic factors that included age, gender, race, ethnicity, nationality, geographic location, intelligence, learning ability/disability, physical ability/disability, psychological ability/disability, religion, sexual orientation, and socioeconomic status. Three groups of students emerged:

- Group I chose all 13 factors as pertinent to their definition of race.
- Group II selected race, ethnicity, and/or nationality or various combinations of the three.

- Group III comprised students who selected various combinations of the 13 bio- and sociodemographic factors but not all of them. Moreover, this group did not include those students grouped in definitions one and two.

Student respondents received no prompting that could have influenced their responses, nor could the instrument itself, because the definitions were asked for before students began to respond to the questionnaire.

In addition to assessing the respondents' definition of diversity, the classroom climate survey measured (a) respondents' background and bio- and sociodemographic information, and (b) respondents' comments on what was working well and suggestions for improving diversity in the classroom. The survey sample involved 10,234 undergraduate and graduate students with an oversampling of students of color. In terms of the sample and population representation, (a) significantly more female undergraduate and graduate students responded to the survey than male; (b) there were variations across colleges in the number of student respondents; and (c) no differences were found for race/ethnicity between the samples of undergraduate and graduate students who responded to the survey.

Among the most significant findings are the following:

1. Respondents' perceptions of classroom climate varied based on how they defined diversity.
2. Respondents treated questions associated with "respectful interactions" in the classroom differently from questions about instruction that equalized diverse students' chances of being successful.
3. Respectful interactions between students and faculty and among students themselves was perceived to occur more in discipline-based courses than in General Education Requirement (GER) courses.
4. Respondents reported that GER courses provided experiences and information that helped them gain a greater understanding of diversity than did their discipline-based courses.
5. A high percentage of all respondents reported the presence of a supportive or very supportive classroom environment for White students and for men. A significantly lower percentage reported the presence of a supportive classroom climate for either students of color or gay and lesbian students.

6. Across most questions in the survey, there were consistent significant differences between African American perceptions and White perceptions of classroom climate, with those of African Americans being lower, and between Hispanic perceptions and White perceptions, with those of Hispanics being lower.
7. The perceptions of White respondents about classroom climate generally were more positive than for any other group except Asians, in some cases.

In summary, this research study suggests that discussions about curricular transformation should include an appropriate line of questioning, consideration of respondents' definition of diversity, and a study that yields a body of baseline data to inform an institution about the effectiveness of newly offered and refined interventions.

Choosing Outcomes: Neutrality Versus Controversy

A campus vision about curricular transformation can open the door to acceptance, and global goals/objectives can begin to solidify the vision. The real work and care of transformation will be enshrined in measurable outcomes statements that guide planning and implementation. Once again, the institutional readiness framework determines selection. A campus that needs to transition developmentally into curricular transformation might select inclusive outcomes *that overlap with more traditional curricular outcomes*. For example, the purpose of curricular expansion could be to:

- expand the content and scholarship within the disciplines;
- support students as they expand and clarify their view of the world;
- create a learning environment that allows students to connect the disciplines;
- facilitate students' ability to create new perspectives on which they can base sound judgments; and/or
- examine the comparative overlap of the fundamental questions raised across varied dimensions.

Even if the emphasis is on traditional curricular change, as opposed to an inclusive curriculum, the outcomes mentioned above would be acceptable to most faculty. A more advanced campus, that is, one that is at an advanced level of readiness, may select outcomes that appear to be more politically charged. Thus, the purpose of curricular expansion might be to:

- destandardize the notion that the universal baseline for experiences, interests, and characteristics is White and male;
- move away from dichotomous and oppositional framing on one or more dimensions (empowered/disenfranchised, rich/poor, Eurocentric/non-Western);
- think of course content in terms of history and politics when appropriate;
- demand a rethinking of the disciplines to incorporate multicultural and multiracial perspectives; and/or
- connect social categories based on hierarchical power relationships.

During the entire sequence of discussions about curricular transformation, the voice of the faculty is not only the *most important*, but also the *most strategic* factor in assuring that (a) a transformed curriculum is infused effectively into the general education curriculum and the discipline-based curriculum, and (b) the commitment to transformation is a long-term goal.

On many campuses the faculty discussion about diversity generally can be a strong indicator of the quality and direction of discourse about curricular transformation. These discussions occur across a range of venues and constituent groups; some are informal and others reach the agenda of formal committee groups and councils. When dissonance about curricular transformation does occur, it often develops because nonfaculty groups, whose members are very committed, instigate for change before and during faculty considerations. Faculty tend to have a different type of conversation, one that emphasizes faculty values, academic freedom, curricular decision making and autonomy, course sequencing, accreditation requirements, teaching demands, and student outcomes. The deliberate process that faculty use in their review of proposed curricular changes may not jibe with the expectations of nonfaculty groups.

Since curricular transformation cannot occur without faculty approval and support, campus leaders must place the decision-making process in the hands of the faculty, who, in turn, will engage in a good-faith consideration of what will produce an inclusive curriculum. The critical discourse can occur within the academic department, in faculty-led committees or councils, and within the faculty senate. The last body offers the opportunity for an interdisciplinary review and discussion and, ultimately, broad acceptance.

Organizing Curricular Transformation Around Key Questions and Issues

Curricular transformation efforts that involve traditional existing courses should be approached somewhat differently from the development of a new course. Traditional courses have evolved around an existing conceptual framework and topics that have accepted value. Thus, the historical expectations of faculty and students must be accounted for as the discussion about refining and reshaping the core components of the course ensues.

The opportunity to introduce new ideas about diversity into a course as a pilot or phased-in approach can serve the interest of all the stakeholders. Faculty members have the opportunity to test, discard, retain, assess, and evaluate proposed course changes. Internal and external review can establish the validity of the infused or enriched academic content and the degree to which it is congruent with the traditional content. However, the politics of how this can or should be done are very important and should be included in a broad campus discussion.

An example of the emergence of a transformational course occurred during the development of the Women and Technology course at North Carolina State University (1999). Dr. Mary Wyer, director of the Women in Science and Engineering Project, piloted her ideas in an existing course, Contemporary Science, Technology, and Human Values (MDS 302). This course was an important trial selection because students who enrolled in it did so to fulfill a general education requirement (Science Technology and Society [STS]), and they understood that the course would use a comparative analysis.

The emerging Women and Technology course would target engineering and computing students as well as Women's Studies students seeking to explore the social influences that shape and are shared by technological change and innovations. An important component of the course is a basic engineering design exercise, and the course is organized around four key issues and questions:

- The mythical absence of women from technological development: Have women been inventors of technologies or merely users? What were women's contributions to technological design and development values?

- The effects of technology on women: How does technology affect women's social and economic status and health? How does it contribute to their liberation or subordination?

- New technologies that have special importance for women: An in-depth look at three areas—reproductive technologies, information technologies, and domestic technologies.

- The effects of women's activities on technological development as consumers, users, voters, and citizens.

Following the successful pilot of the course, the syllabus was refined, restructured, and submitted through the program, departmental, and college processes to secure its availability for STS credit on a permanent basis.

Diversity and Teaching for Inquiry

Several years ago, North Carolina State University committed to several major initiatives that would have a significant impact on undergraduate education. One initiative, the Alcoa Project, provided resource support and release time from teaching for faculty who wanted to incorporate diversity into the curricular content and instructional method of an existing course. I served as codirector of the project, along with Dr. Rebecca Leonard. As a part of the project, the faculty member was paired with a graduate teaching assistant or another faculty member. A second initiative, Inquiry-Guided Learning (IGL), sought to create a community of faculty whose members were committed to acquiring instructional skills that would promote active learning, critical thinking, and student responsibility for learning. Lee (2004) summarizes the development of IGL and offers several discipline-based examples of its application in her book, *Teaching and Learning Through Inquiry: A Guidebook for Institutions and Instructors*.

Although both initiatives evolved independently, a timely occurrence contributed to their ultimate merger. Some of the same faculty were involved in both projects as well as a third initiative that emphasized student learning outcomes assessment. Curricular transformation tends to focus on a diversity-based infusion of the course content. At many institutions this is attempted without addressing a commensurate issue: students may or may not have the analytical tools to make the necessary conceptual and cognitive connections that are expected in a transformed course. Thus, as faculty participated in the Alcoa Project, they were encouraged as well to consider -giving attention to measurable learning outcomes and the subsequent assessment of the impact of the project on student learning.

What we learned at North Carolina State University was that the cumulative effect of linking curricular transformation to teaching for inquiry, and then to student learning outcomes assessment, produced a dynamic interaction that would not have resulted from an emphasis on any one area. The following examples outline how this interaction occurred in several courses.

Introduction to Physical Chemistry (CH331)

Dr. Laura Sremanick—Faculty Instructor
Ms. Sheila Maness—Graduate Teaching Assistant

Generally, challenging upper-level sciences courses are not seen as worthy prospects for a curricular transformation project. The dual demands of conceptual understanding and problem solving present difficulties for many students. This one-semester physical chemistry course is taken primarily by junior- and senior-level students from three different majors: biochemistry, pulp and paper technology, and a bachelor of arts in chemistry. We chose this course because of the availability of a problem session that afforded the instructor more time to test ideas and strategies, and, second, the foundations established in the course (with its broad scope) can apply to an array of other physical chemistry courses.

Course Objectives

- Cultivating the cognitive and affective domains—attempts to account for varied student learning styles, and seeks to create a heightened awareness of different attitudes toward the course and other students.
- Creating an awareness of student responsibility for learning— attempts to instill in the student a sense of ownership of the course.
- Incorporating a historical context to course material—attempts to establish the importance of the contributions of all people, especially those from underrepresented groups, to the field of physical chemistry.

- Translating abstract ideas into an understandable format—attempts to move students away from over-reliance on memorization and low levels of comprehension to an expansion of thinking that includes comprehension of abstract ideas and the assumptions inherent in them.
- Using case studies to establish relevance to students' disciplinary interest—case studies provide more relevance for chemistry majors and nonchemistry majors and allow for course material to be presented in terms of real-life applications.

Implementation Strategies

The following strategies were identified as the most feasible to complement the five course objectives.

1. Provide alterations in the current teaching practices to target different learning styles and enhance development of the cognitive domain.
2. Use pre- and post-course surveys to gauge progress in the affective domain.
3. Design individual course contracts with student input that emphasizes student responsibility and ownership and allows students to design their own grading scheme.
4. Prepare, for example, a self-written course pack that includes writing assignments to incorporate a historical context to supplement other classroom materials.
5. Determine the progress of students toward understanding abstract ideas and recognizing assumptions by using exams, quizzes, and group problem assignments.
6. Introduce case studies at relevant points during the presentation of the course material whose content reflects real-world issues and links to students' disciplinary interests.

Assessment

One of the core assumptions associated with this project is that different teaching methods can positively affect the various learning styles of students. Student and peer evaluations can be used to assess teaching effectiveness. Various student attitudes toward the course can be gauged through pre- and post-course surveys, and throughout the course, with classroom assessment techniques. Student performance on tests and group problem-solving sessions should emphasize knowledge of the course content and the learning outcomes associated with the course objectives.

Science courses do not often lend themselves to the same type of curricular transformation as do courses in liberal arts and social sciences. While the latter areas can draw from a growing body of nontraditional and diverse scholarship, science and math-related projects can emphasize the diversity of students' cognitive styles and learning styles and/or the diversity of the learning environments.

Sociology of the Family (SOC204)

Dr. Maxine Atkinson—Faculty Instructor
Jason Joyner—Graduate Teaching Assistant

This course was selected as a target for curriculum transformation because it is a "bread and butter" course that generates high enrollment, and because other upper-level courses (undergraduate and graduate) incorporate the core concepts of family.

Course Objectives

There were two primary objectives for this project. First, the collaborators wanted to address more effectively race and sexual orientation issues in the class, and by doing so enhance the inclusive nature of the course. Before developing this project, the collaborators felt comfortable with the manner and degree in which class and gender issues were covered in the course. There was some concern, however, that race had been addressed haphazardly and issues of sexual orientation not at all. The second objective evolved from a concern that visual learners might have less of an advantage because of the paucity of visual aids. Despite the emphasis on an inclusive mode of instruction, and a transition away from lecture-based teaching, the historical tendency had been to ignore the needs of visual learners.

Desired Learning Outcomes

Three primary learning outcomes are associated with this project:

1. Students will be able to conceptualize and explain the interlocking relationship among race, class, gender, and sexual orientation.

2. Students will evidence an understanding of how social inequities are connected to forms of social organization and systems of meaning.

3. Students will discover how social inequalities are produced and maintained and what their consequences are for people's life chances.

Implementation Strategies

The primary focus is on promoting active learning strategies among students that will focus attention on the relationship among various forms of diversity, privilege, and oppression. Active learning strategies encourage students to think reflectively about the course content, to ask and answer questions at different levels of questioning (Bloom's Taxonomy), and to offer well-reasoned arguments for the positions they take. Topics are introduced in ways that generate substantive conversation while minimizing student resistance. The instructors have developed a bank of overheads for use as needed to illustrate the difficult ideas often encountered in this course and similar classes.

Assessment

The instructors had several ways of assessing students' understanding of the effects of race/ethnicity. The data analysis module requires that students construct a bivariate table, with race as the predictor variable and family structure as the outcome variable. Then they add a control variable for family income. What they see is that, once one controls for income, there is less difference in family structure for the richer families and a bigger difference for poorer families. They also read an article on the effect of racism on family structure that should help them interpret the data. Most students can interpret the data correctly, but few can adequately integrate the literature with the data.

The use of two films—one a 20-minute news program, the other a full-length feature film—is more effective at helping students understand race/ethnicity. Most students use the films as evidence of the effect of race on family and individual behavior. When given a choice of types of evidence to cite, they are far more likely to cite these visual forms of data than they are the statistical data.

The instructor found that adding sexuality to the course's focus was not a good idea. Students were happy to talk and read about sexuality, but though class discussions were heated, students' comments were less analytical and more emotional.

When the instructors compared answers about social class to answers about sexuality, there were marked differences. Students used evidence to back up their assertions about social class; however, when they moved to discussions about sexuality, they cited much less evidence used and referred to the Bible far more frequently.

At the undergraduate level, the instructors began to teach in the first-year inquiry seminar program only. Based on experience with mixed-level classes, the instructors decided to concentrate on beefing up the race section of the course and excluding sexuality. They added readings, two films, a data analysis module, and an experiential exercise at a shopping mall.

Cross-Cultural Technology Transfer (MDS 848 and HONORS 296)

Dr. David Greene—Course Coordinator
Dr. Phillip Tavakoli—Course Coordinator

The last decade has seen a proliferation in globalization of technology. While the commercial and entrepreneurial aspects of technology transfer are evident, what isn't clear is the relation between technology and values, especially cultural values. An interdisciplinary course on Cross-Cultural Technology Transfer challenged students to address this issue. The course targeted students who expressed an interest in any form of international organization, business, and politics. The course also drew well from the College of Natural Resources and the College of Management.

The course was shaped around the critical analysis of questions and topics. When technology transfers from one culture to another, does the definition of "technology" change? Is the transfer always from more- to less-developed people? How is respect maintained for the culture to which the technology is transferred? When transfer occurs, what are the criteria for success? How do concepts such as globalization and "sustainable development" shape the meaning of cross-cultural technology transfer?

Readings and Case Studies

Students in this course are introduced to a range of topics though readings, case studies, and guest lectures. For example, among the case study topics on the course syllabus are:

- Agricultural Technology and Research Transfer after World War II and during the Green revolutions: India, Philippines, Peru, Mexico

- Agro-forestry in Northeast India: America's role as a partner
- Dependence and Interdependence in Technology Transfer
- Water: Issues in an Islamic context: Egypt. Reports from students who were there
- Energy: Improved cooking stoves in Nepal
- Transfer of Germanic Forest Management Philosophy to other European Countries and From There Into African and Asian colonies
- Protected Forest Area Systems: Integrating Parks and People

Course Objective

Students will learn to do critical thinking and analysis about the underlying principles, optimum methods, and effects of technology transfer from a developed country to a developing country with a different cultural tradition.

Learning Outcomes

Student will accomplish the following:

- Learn the diverse objectives for technology transfer as it relates to industry, natural resources, financial institutions, and information technology.
- Learn the diverse criteria for measuring the success of a transfer, and see how these criteria diverge depending on whether one takes into account gender, environmental, social, and cultural issues as well as economic and political ones.
- Learn the relevance of cultural traditions, the current socioeconomic situations, and environmental factors to the criteria for assessing technology transfers.
- Learn the relevance of the conflict between the principles and assumptions of liberal democracies and those of religious, political, or cultural fundamentalist countries for the technology transfer process.
- Learn the common reasons why technology transfer fails.

Course Justification and Appeal

While learning outcomes evolve from the beginning of a course to the end, students may not perceive the immediate relevancy or value of a transformed course. Consequently, the course coordinators provide several career-related justifications for taking the course that may have an immediate appeal to student's interests.

This course will appeal to students who:

- Envision a career in international nongovernmental organizations, international financial institutions, diplomatic missions, and church groups that play a key role in technology transfer.
- Are planning to join the Peace Corps after graduation and need exposure to the aforementioned learning outcomes.
- Have had a meaningful study-abroad experience and often express a desire to follow through on their newly acquired internationalized consciousness by looking at issues that relate that experience to their future endeavors.
- Are learning new uses for technologies and who may serve in companies where exploring that technology is a strong possibility.
- Are preparing for leadership roles in technology transfer and need experience in thinking about the complex issues associated with that area.
- Seek to apply a liberal arts framework to the study of technology transfer.

Implementation Strategies

Students were exposed to presentations by outside experts, and significant time was allotted for questions and answers. They also read and discussed case studies and reflected on their level of involvement in these two strategies.

Assessment

To foster student engagement and reflection, the course coordinators required students to submit regular reports that included questions, critical reflections, and summaries of class discussion, which are graded. Students were also expected to give presentations, write papers, and complete one quiz.

Guidelines for Implementing Faculty Senate Resolution on Cultural and Ethnic Diversity at the University of Washington

The University of Washington's Faculty Council on Academic Standards developed a set of guidelines to assist academic departments in conducting curricular reviews and submitting plans for curriculum development. The guidelines accompanied a formal Resolution on Cultural Lines and Ethnic Diversity that identified a broad learning goal—development of critical thinking skills in cultural and ethnic diversity. The guidelines did not establish a single standard of evaluation; instead, they attempted to define relevant learning outcomes for cultural diversity that were consistent with new and emerging scholarship across disciplines and with educational practice nationally and locally. Few institutions, either two- or four-year, have the benefit of the vision and proactive strategies that are developed by a faculty-led governing body. Support for curricular transformation by a faculty senate lends a high degree of validity to the critical discourse that can easily get bogged down in political morass.

Emphasizing Learning Outcomes

To their credit, the faculty senate maintained its focus on the learning outcomes that should or will result from curricular transformation. Their contention is that such outcomes not only facilitate students' learning in the discipline, but they also prepare students to make wise choices about what to believe and what to do once they leave the institution. A focus on outcomes allows for application of formal assessment tools, which, in turn, facilitates evidence-based decision making. The faculty senate offered the following as examples of possible learning outcomes for departmental courses on cultural and ethnic diversity:

- Examine the social construction of identities by race, gender, ethnicity, class, sexual orientation, etc.
- Recognize various forms of stereotyping, prejudice, privilege, and discrimination.
- Understand cultural differences in identity development.
- Distinguish between individual responsibility and structural barriers to choice and opportunity.
- Distinguish facts, cultural assumptions, interpretations, and opinions relating to issues of diversity.
- Understand disciplinary approaches in framing and analyzing problems and issues regarding cultural diversity.
- Take a supportable position in the face of irreconcilable cultural differences.

- Think about complex issues from different cultural perspectives.
- Differentiate between personal discomfort and intellectual disagreement in cultural conflict situations.

This list is not exhaustive; it is meant only to provide a starting point for departmental reviews. The outcomes do reflect, conceptually, faculty's perceptions of the nature of the type of critical thinking that is necessary in multicultural settings. The outcomes are also written in a manner that emphasizes active learning.

Suggestions for Conducting a Departmental Review

The faculty senate at the University of Washington recognized that there was significant variation in how departments, schools, and colleges approached review and development of plans for curriculum development, both the general curriculum and the transformed curriculum. Some departments may prefer to infuse into existing courses; others may want to create new courses. Departments that are already vested in a significant number of courses that enhance students' ability to think critically about diversity may wish to create a more advanced or comprehensive curricula.

Departments were offered a set of guiding questions that would be useful in understanding a review of courses that teach students to think critically about diversity and about developing plans for change:

1. What diversity issues exist in the department's fields of study?
2. What have other departments in similar institutions done, and what success have they had?
3. What concepts and skills related to cultural diversity are currently taught in introductory courses or in the major?
4. What are the department's goals in teaching about cultural and ethnic diversity? Are they being met?
5. How can the department curriculum in this area be improved?
6. What resources are needed to strengthen the departmental curriculum?

The Curriculum Project at the University of Washington represented a thoughtful, inclusive, and systematic initiative that cultivated buy-in from the most important stakeholders. Participation of the faculty in general and the faculty senate in particular contributed to the robust nature of the initiative and, ultimately, to its sustainability.

A Consonance of Outcomes

Developing meaningful and measurable learning outcomes is a critical component of effective classroom assessment. While many faculty members include course objectives on the syllabi they distribute to students, they generally don't include learning outcomes because the faculty may not be expert in assessing either the quality of teaching or the impact on student learning. Outcome statements can serve a valuable purpose: they can suggest to the developer the kinds of strategic questions that need to be asked about the teaching strategies and classroom dynamics that need to be considered. Because diversity has not been a consistent component of campus conversations on teaching and learning, it is reasonable to assume that it also has not been addressed significantly among faculty in conversations about outcomes assessment. The example below may shed some light on the value of developing concrete diversity outcomes and the kinds of questions that can influence faculty considerations.

Learning outcome statement: to use reflection to encourage students to make connections between traditional course content in the disciplines and to encourage their inclusion of diversity/globalism outcomes.

Questions faculty might consider:

1. What instructional strategies associated with reflection (reflective thinking) do I want to use?
2. What new knowledge or competencies should emerge from the "connections" students make?
3. Should I incorporate writing experiences, and, if so, which ones are appropriate?
4. Which traditional content area offers the most fertile ground to incorporate diversity/globalism outcomes?
5. Should I incorporate moral/ethical considerations and/or examples that are relevant to the students' experience?
6. Should students be allowed to use their personal/subjective experiences to facilitate the "connections"?

7. What pedagogical tool will best accomplish this?
8. What is the proper balance in the course between traditional and nontraditional scholarship?
9. What ground rules will help students negotiate ambiguity or controversy?
10. To what degree should I as the instructor allow an inclusive curriculum to interpret traditional course content in terms of history or politics?

There is a dynamic relationship between the learning outcome and the questions for consideration, with each causing reflection about the other and, ultimately, refinement of the teaching and learning process. Student outcomes (academic performance, learning, success in the major, etc.) do not occur in a vacuum but are affected by the execution of well-developed faculty outcomes. The following example characterizes this relationship.

Instructional outcome for faculty: to be sensitive to the linguistic and conceptual demands of class discussions and activities so that diverse students are not pushed to communicate beyond their level of proficiency or conceptualize beyond their level of intellectual maturity.

Instructional strategies

1. Review theories and models of learning that address diverse learning styles and strategies and discipline-specific best practices.
2. Participate in faculty development workshops (if available) that bolster one's ability to address student literacy challenges.
3. Sample student skills and competencies (writing, thinking, information processing, etc.) and establish performance baselines.
4. Use discussion groups that transition diverse learners through different levels:
   • informational discussions that allow students to interject subjective opinions and affective considerations;
   • moderately challenging discussions and assignments whose purpose is to scaffold basic skills and competencies upward to higher levels; and
   • higher-ordered discussions that incorporate guided questions (modeled by the instructor) and move on to increased reliance on student-generated questions.

5. Facilitate student preparedness for each lecture by using a structured format that involves pre-prepared questions or a discussion worksheet (see example by Craig Nelson in chapter 4).

6. Rotate students in cooperative peer groups and ask them to self-evaluate own work, write one-page summaries of assignments, and evaluate peer work (anonymously) online (for examples, see Cooper, Robinson, & Ball, 2003).

The optimal paradigm would be to synchronize student learning outcomes, faculty instructional outcomes, lines of questioning, and instructional strategies that reflect the last three factors. Such a tailored effort, while difficult to achieve, can represent the kind of performance target that produces benefits for students and faculty anywhere along the process while maintaining high levels of quality. Such a paradigm cannot evolve without an intentional and well-supported structure that reflects the values of the faculty and the support of institutional leadership.

For many faculty, the intersection of goals, objectives, and outcomes with diversity, globalism, curricular and pedagogical transformation, and classroom climate is not only a new endeavor but one that, conceptually, can appear to lack both clarity and coherence. Thus, it might be valuable to provide a visual or graphic that summarizes information in a meaningful way (see Figure 6.1).

The diversity matrix in Figure 6.1 could be inserted into a faculty development training initiative to allow faculty to practice writing outcomes under different topical categories. One column or one row could be completed, and faculty could work collaboratively to finish the matrix. Administrators, faculty, students, and staff could work to develop a consensus about entries across a row (university/college outcomes), or faculty from different disciplines could complete a row that would reflect outcomes in the core curriculum or general education curriculum. Faculty will need the most assistance with the row that requires constructing evidence that supports attainment of a program objective/outcome or, more difficult, learning outcomes. In an earlier chapter I discussed the problems that arise when institutions generate diversity initiatives without a conceptual model. Similar difficulties or problems occur when measurable outcomes are absent. As an assessment tool, a matrix conveys a visual imprint to users that is a result of their constructive conversations and systematic thinking.

FIGURE 6.1
Diversity Matrix

	Diversity Outcomes	Global Outcomes	Curriculum Transformation	Pedagogical Transformation	Classroom Climate
University/College Goals/Objectives Outcomes		Students will understand the effect of diverse religious values.	To expose all students to the significance of diversity across disciplines.		
Department/Program Goals/Objectives Outcomes		Students will produce a comparative analysis of three articles on globalism.	To develop a 12-credit-hour diversity requirement in the major.		
Course Objectives/Outcomes		Grades will be higher in those sections with transformed curriculum than those in a non-transformed one.	Students will exhibit inquiry-guided learning outcomes in diversity-enhanced courses.		
Evidence of Achieved Outcome		Employers will report that graduates are global communicators.	Using a pre-post assessment, faculty will exhibit more substantive knowledge about diversity.		

References

Cooper, J. L., Robinson, P., & Ball, D. (2003). *Small group instruction in higher education: Lessons from the past, visions of the future.* Stillwater, OK: New Forums Press.

Lee, V. (2004). *Teaching and learning through inquiry.* Sterling, VA: Stylus.

7

EMPOWERING THE VOICE OF DIVERSE STUDENTS IN THE COLLEGE CLASSROOM

While many instructors seek to achieve a range of curricular objectives and learning outcomes in a particular course, some confront emotionally charged conflicts between students or between students and instructors who are polarized along ideological, political, and/or religious fault lines. Even an instructor's most reasoned and articulate explanation of course objectives (engagement, intellectual inquiry, cooperative learning, etc.) can become secondary to students' perceptions of course content, or classroom interactions that challenge their beliefs. For faculty members (and administrators), few things are more frustrating than refereeing students or student groups because they do not disagree respectfully. Even more unsettling are the scenarios in which an instructor becomes the catalyst for classroom confrontation. One expected outcome of such situations is that many students choose to mute or camouflage their "voices" because of fear of retaliation or being stigmatized.

One could argue that a causal relationship exists between the concept of student academic freedom and the expression of students' voices. Students should be free to engage in inquiry-guided learning, learn from their mistakes, study, speculate, evaluate, and understand. They should also be free from intimidation and indoctrination by their peers or faculty members when they express their beliefs, ideas, or perspectives. However, the student voice can mature best when there is some structure and regulation in the classroom that promotes constructive dialogue. In his discussion of the historical roots of academic freedom for students, Pavela (2006) notes that "speech codes may serve the primary purpose of diverting attention from more substantive issues of inclusion and civility" (p. B8). The parameters for collaboration and critical discourse must be explicit, understood, practiced, and affirmed. Early in their undergraduate careers, students should begin to understand that their individual responsibility for learning includes supporting a positive classroom climate for their benefit and the benefit of others.

Factors That Facilitate Student Voices

Earlier chapters have suggested why systematic incorporation of diversity into all levels of campus culture is both a challenge and an enormous opportunity. From the perspectives of many diverse and nontraditional students, beginning college is demanding and involves navigational skills, through ambiguous or threatening territory, and a desire to integrate into unfamiliar groups and settings. At times, diverse students can feel that limiting public expression of their beliefs, feelings, and perceptions might be best. However, learning occurs best in dynamic and supportive environments, and the potential fallout from restricted participation can have negative consequences in the short and long term. Instructors should consider designing course objectives and related strategies that affirm students as participants in the learning environment.

One theoretical construct that offers a valuable perspective on student readiness to cope with the stressors of a new and changing environment is the concept of "hardiness." Kobasa (1979) describes a healthy person as one who welcomes, and thrives, during periods of stress. He or she exhibits a personality style that not only influences ways of thinking and feeling, but also encourages assertive behavior and risk taking. For diverse students this can translate into a greater willingness to express their "voice," especially in academic settings. Hardiness is framed in the context of three integrated components: commitment, challenge, and control (Lifton, Seay, & Bushko, 2004, p. 104). Students express a sense of commitment, which reflects a sense of value and meaningfulness, when they become deeply involved in activities, classes, and relationships. Challenge demands a willingness to experience and grow amid new circumstances. Hardy students respond to challenges by looking for answers or alternative options. The component that perhaps is most important to student voices is control: The belief that they influence the outcomes that occur in their lives. Students who believe that external factors influence most of their life tend to lack confidence in their own voice.

The goals and aspirations that motivate diverse students to attend college seem to reflect more similarities with majority students than they do differences, thus they are not as significant in affecting the voice of the student as actual events that occur once they enroll. Motivational factors do have predictive value and frequently play a role in admissions decisions.

Hardiness and Confidence: A Comparative Example

I recently asked myself the question: As a person of color, why do I feel comfortable communicating across different contexts and with varied groups in higher education circles? I also posed a related question: Why do many diverse and nontraditional students report feeling isolated, estranged, and muted on their respective campuses and in college classrooms? Excluding for the moment my age and years of tenure within academic environments, I wondered if there were common factors that might explain my facility and their discomfort. Using the students' situation as a frame of reference, my introspective analysis yielded the following about my comfort zone compared to theirs:

- I draw strengths from the knowledge base that I have developed in my discipline and in the topical areas associated with my research and administrative responsibilities. The cumulative result is that I can move comfortably across boundaries. In the early stages of their academic careers, diverse students may not have developed a similar confidence level, even when they are mastering academic work.
- I have learned (and understand the value of) the "shared language" used in the formal and informal discourse that permeates communication within the academy. Students from nontraditional backgrounds who may exhibit varied communication styles are challenged because their early collegiate experiences don't affirm their "voice" as an asset, and it is assumed that they will adapt to the expectations of traditional learning environments.
- Diverse students, staff, and faculty often experience some type of stress and ambiguity associated with the politics of difference, and this includes perceptions as well as actual experiences. With the support

of a strong cadre of student peers, majority and minority, in college and later from committed advocates, I developed coping skills to neutralize the potential impact of negative experiences. While the mere presence of diversity as an environmental factor is important, the quality and quantity of experiences and interactions, with those whose diversity made a difference in an academic setting, had a significant impact on my life. A Caucasian history professor facilitated my identity development, as well as that of my African American peers, in a course on the history of Africa. Members of that group, in turn, became organizational leaders on campus. If diverse students don't receive similar support, they may be slow to cultivate a sense of security as they encounter new contexts and situations.

- There is a clear difference between frequent interactions and productive linkages. As a student leader, I learned this early in my career, and over the years I have continued to promote effective partnerships. Students can come together in a study group (a peer interaction), but if they do not use effective learning strategies, that linkage will not be productive. Two of the most successful Minority Engineering Programs are at the University of Michigan and Carnegie Mellon University. The study and problem-solving groups at these institutions encourage the acquisition of analytical tools that are appropriate for the academic content being covered. Students of color do not come together in nonproductive study groups in either program. Intentional efforts must be made to involve diverse students in linkages that enhance their confidence levels, especially when interacting with majority students, staff, and faculty.

- Majority (White) students who emigrate from homogeneous communities and educational backgrounds to college campuses that replicate their personal experiences are offered opportunities to adjust to the culture of college. Every affirming experience within this culture contributes to the development of their identity. Diverse students may face the challenge of developing multiple identities in environments that reinforce and reward traditional behaviors but demean and/or devalue nontraditional ones. For example, during my graduate years, I was expected to adopt the traditional identity of an Ivy League student in a traditional psychology program. At the same time, I was a mentor for minority undergraduates and an active leader in the Black

Graduate Student Association. I simply have more years of practice than do diverse students at consolidating identity development, but I share their awareness of the stress involved with this process over time. Even at my level of development, I must stay attuned to the cues that tell me when I must incorporate one or more aspects of a traditional identity in response to real or imagined stressors.

Social Anxiety: Racial-Ethnic Differences

Another explanation for the manner in which student groups negotiate the stress of encountering new environments refers to the anxiety that results from the prospect or presence of personal evaluation in real or imagined situations. Such feelings are referred to as social anxiety (Schlenker & Leary, 1982). Social anxiety affects what kinds of impression others form of an individual and how that individual chooses to manage those impressions. Various researchers have suggested a relationship between social anxiety and racial-ethnic group membership. Okazaki (1997) examined social anxiety among Asian Americans, and White (1991) suggested a historical basis for African Americans' tolerance of stress and its relationship to anxiety. Asians and Asian Americans value education highly and view academic achievement as a prerequisite for success and as a coping mechanism to deal with discrimination. African Americans have a longer and more brutal history of discrimination in this country that affects every aspect of their lives. So much of their energy has been spent coping with an overwhelming amount of emotional stress, even as they seek to accomplish positive educational outcomes. Garcia-Preto (1982) proposed higher levels of social anxiety among Hispanic Americans, who perceive a significant degree of cultural- and language-based estrangement in educational settings and in the country as a whole. Hispanic students who are first-generation college students and who use English as a second language may not expect the same level of social mobility or educational success as do many other groups. In the last two decades, more academic and social educational supports have emerged that should help to reduce the amount of social anxiety for Hispanic students.

LeSure-Lester and King (2005, p. 360) note that previous studies have examined differences in social anxiety between a specific racial-ethnic group and White students; participants were drawn from four-year colleges. Their study examined the variations among four ethnic groups (African American,

Asian American, Hispanic American and White American) in two-year colleges. Study participants responded to the Social Anxiety Thoughts Questionnaire, which measures the frequency of cognitions that accompany social distress and anxiety. The results indicated that there are racial-ethnic differences in the experience of social anxiety, but the findings must be viewed in the context of a self-report of social anxiety—not actual distressful behaviors. Self-reported anxiety that does not have, or is not triggered by, an actual distressor (death, tragedy, suspension, harassment, etc.) is less valid than when a direct stimulus elicits the actual anxiety.

A Student Voice and Intercultural Development

Earlier, I referred to classroom structure as a critical dimension in the expression of students' voices. Structure allows for an integration of academic content and the student perspective and facilitates students' participation as they navigate differences in the college classroom. Structure can refer to the active strategies that an instructor incorporates to empower student engagement over time, with the academic content and with one another. Bennett and Bennett (2004) offer a six-stage developmental model of intercultural sensitivity and adaptation that could provide a usable conceptual framework. Her model provides both a generic application to classroom interactions and communication and more specific attention to diversity and cultural differences.

Bennett's Developmental Model of Intercultural Sensitivity begins with three ethnocentric stages (denial, defense, and minimization) in which a person's own culture becomes the primary filter through which he or she interprets and experiences reality. Thus, in the college classroom some students either neglect to notice differences or they think in extremely simple categories (denial); some develop a perspective about differences that distinguishes between "us" and "them" (defense); and some minimize all differences and suggest that everyone is the same in some universal context (minimization). Each perspective suggests a motivational basis for students' expressions of "voice," yet none genuinely seeks to accept, understand, and value differences. Moreover, because students are locked into a particular developmental stage, they limit their ability to adapt to other situational contexts and other developmental stages that may impose greater demands.

As individuals become increasingly more aware of cultural differences, they move into ethnorelative stages (acceptance, adaptation, integration) in which they recognize and interpret other cultures as different from their own, and they tend to make evaluative judgments about such differences. Bennett suggests that this may be the first time many see the complexity and validity of another culture's worldview. Applying the advanced stages of the developmental model to the college classroom and the expression of voice, some students make more complicated observations about behavioral differences and connect them to value differences (acceptance); some students are motivated to progress from knowing about differences to developing skill sets that facilitate effective interactions with other cultures (adaptation); and some students internalize the core aspects of two or more cultural identities over time and develop a strong sense of biculturalism (integration).

Students in the last three stages have strengthened their filter of interpretation and their comfort zone in situations involving intercultural engagement. Their voices are influenced by intellectual curiosity, introspective integrity, adaptive expertise, interpersonal sensitivity, and a fundamental desire to make sense of the world both on- and off-campus. Movement through these stages of development is more fluid and meets with greater success when the process is contained in a context that reduces anxiety, encourages learning, and supports peer engagement—in other words, when we use classroom strategies and innovative pedagogies that convert theoretical models into viable learning outcomes. The following examples can shed light on this important conversion.

Academic Discourse Communities

Many colleges and universities have invested in varied programs that address the needs of entering students in general and specific populations in particular. As might be expected, such programs have varied purposes; some have only surface impact, and others are more intrusive. In the case of diverse and nontraditional students, it is important to expose students to academic and cocurricular experiences, for which they perceive not only educational value but also the presence of equity and a respect for differences. Classroom climates that encourage students to engage course content while also being allowed—in fact, encouraged—to express divergent viewpoints promote sustained dialogue and, ultimately, intellectual development. Jalomo and Rendon (2004, p. 38) identify two critical processes that facilitate the transition to college for diverse students especially students of color: validation and involvement. The absence of such processes can negatively affect students' academic interactions with faculty, social experiences on campus, academic and intellectual development, and commitment to the institution, all of which are considered important to student retention (Rendon, Garcia, & Person, 2004).

Laura Rendon (1994) a committed champion for diversity, defines validation as a confirmation process in which the institution and its agents (faculty, staff, and administrators) initiate the experiences that support and confirm the identity, development, and success of students of color. Of utmost importance is that validation must empower the student as a learner and must strengthen the student's sense of self and comfort with multiple identities. Short-term, one-time, or poorly conceptualized activities cannot accomplish this, and programs that do not use formative assessment often misperceive the actual impact of their efforts.

Validation becomes functional and effective when students are involved in activities and experiences that link them to the culture of college, that present them as competent peers to others, that offer the opportunity for growth and development, and that allow them to visualize realistically the incremental steps to success. Academic Discourse Communities (ADCs) represent the type of challenging structure that fosters such positive student outcomes as validation and involvement (Osei-Kofi, Richards, & Smith, 2004). The authors offer several examples of pedagogical techniques that facilitate student learning and engagement. Among these are the following:

1. The instructors should incorporate strategies that encourage questioning, critique, and interrogation. Students could practice the development of such skills as they review case studies or scenarios that address contemporary and/or controversial topics. The important ground rule for the class is that no student voice is criticized or stifled, and students should agree to this in writing. Mooney, Fordham, and Lehr (2005, p. 225) describe the faculty development program at St. Lawrence University in oral communication that promotes and enhances teaching strategies and philosophies for productive and civil classroom discourse. The formal program is the Oral Communication Institute, which provides a sustained forum for faculty to explore the relationship among oral communication, critical thinking, and deep learning among students. OCI faculty participants discuss with

each other the multiple ways their classrooms could become communication environments. As OCI faculty explore both social and institutional obstacles that might affect difficult dialogues, they can read Tannen's (1998) book: *The Argument Culture*. Perhaps most important, faculty are expected to provide learning environments that encourage student confidence and competence in extemporaneous and deliberate discourse, especially when the topics for discussion are controversial or politically charged.

2. The instructor can include course matter and content that intentionally evoke varied emotional responses to encourage students to challenge their assumptions about the world. Again, ground rules permit students to express subjective and personal statements as they explore the subject matter. While some instructors recoil from the thought of promoting conflict, others accept that inclusive classrooms can use such situations as powerful learning opportunities when they are managed effectively. On most campuses the core or general education curriculum represents one vehicle for students to develop communication competencies. One or more faculty can develop a curriculum that promotes difficult dialogues among diverse students on sensitive topics. Dr. Jennifer Stromer-Galley, an assistant professor in the Department of Communication at the University at Albany, uses the oral discourse requirement as a unique opportunity for students to discuss and to explore the conflicts that arise between religious and secular society. The goal of the curriculum is to teach students how to participate in a dialogue with well-reasoned arguments and how to listen and respond reasonably and rationally to opinions with which they might disagree. The students entertain a central question: Should colleges and universities promote religious expression on campus, and if so, how should that expression be fostered? Students read position papers generated by members of the campus community who have a stake in this issue—the Muslim Student Association, the Judaic Studies Department, a Christian conservative group, members of the Interfaith Center, etc. The position papers articulate a range of perspectives on this complex question.

3. The instructor should clarify the learning goals and curricular objectives, which include the use of diverse student voices, perspectives, and scholarship. For example, I chose to incorporate all three areas

as teaching strategies in a general psychology course. My curricular objective was to expose students to the importance of gender as a lens of analysis. To encourage them to express their individual voices, I asked each student to describe the last time he or she had made a behavioral observation associated with gender about someone the student knew, and to provide a basis for the statement. To encourage male and female students to express their perspectives, they were required to write short papers and defend the perspective of the opposite sex in support of some sex -role stereotype. To expose the class to diverse scholarship, I selected a topic that offered varied theoretical explanations, and students, in small groups, researched the topics that underscored their scholarly examination. To the degree possible, I selected topics and information that were meaningful and relevant to the student experience and that could be interpreted in various ways.

Several researchers have focused on the impact and power of students' description of their own learning in the context of reflective conversations with other students or with instructors. Rodgers (2006) suggests that the barriers students face while engaging in instructive dialogues can be reduced using descriptive feedback that is neither evaluative or judgmental. Students engage in conversations and describe their cognitive and affective responses as learners relative to a specific learning experience. Rodgers (p. 215) highlights four phases of reflection that can be used:

- presence in experience: learning to see in the moment;
- description of experience: learning through description;
- analysis of experience: learning to think critically and to create theory; and
- experimentation (the next experience): learning to take intelligent action.

Descriptive feedback offers a structure in which students listen analytically to the descriptive experiences and distinctions that emerge in critical dialogues with one another and with the instructor. As a process this can provide students with a sense of authorization and validation about their own truths.

Controversial Topics and Difficult Discourse

When curricular context and classroom discussion allow students to identify and discuss their core beliefs or values, it is critically important that the tone, quality, and outcomes associated with learning continue to be priorities. The key often involves the balance between supporting the student voice and maintaining beneficial structure that promotes positive outcomes.

Siefert and Butler (1993) ask students to develop journals about sensitive concepts and questions. As students learn more, they are better able to examine their own ideas and present well-reasoned arguments to defend their position. For example, for the concepts of feminism, gay rights, genocide, comparable worth, affirmative action, and accountability, students are required to address the following questions in a journal format.

- Define the meaning of the aforementioned key concepts in your own terms.
- How do you feel about each concept and why? The purpose is to examine ideas and present your values. What is the origin of your values, and are you still influenced by that origin?

Students often don't want to defend a controversial position or present well-reasoned arguments in support of topics associated with diversity for a number of reasons: their unfamiliarity with the topic, they don't possess conviction about too many things, doing so would conflict with the major campus values, they fear the consequence of being publicly "outed" for supporting or criticizing diversity, they are not sure how intellectual discourse works, and they are conditioned to seek out comfortable positions where a simple choice will solve the problem (Cioffi, 2005, p. B7). While it is easier for students to offer solutions with simplistic statements ("I believe/support the position because I am conservative or liberal, Republican or Democrat or libertarian, Christian or Muslim or Jewish," etc.), such approaches do not increase their cognitive complexity or depth of understanding.

Pond (2004, p. 37) describes the structured approach he uses in the course, "Controversial Issues in Psychology (PSY 201)." Recognizing the imbalance and ambiguity that often results when students are unprepared to cope with controversial topics and debates, the course is taught based on the principles of inquiry-guided learning and offers special instruction in critical thinking. Pond draws from a wide range of content areas to select controversial issues so that students develop, employ, refine, and practice systematic searching skills that apply to other subjects in psychology, and even other disciplines. Of particular interest is the four-step cycle that students use as they cover controversial issues:

1. Students review background information on the issue to stimulate interest and to help them select an appropriate initial line of inquiry into the controversy.
2. Students assemble in groups to share and analyze additional information they have gathered relevant to the controversy, and they decide how to refine and extend the research topic further.
3. Groups exchange information with one another and try to establish a clear understanding of the controversy.
4. Groups state and explain their positions and share them with the class. Sometimes students debate in an online forum. Pond gives a multiple-choice quiz in this final stage to assess how well students understand the main points of opposing arguments.

Periodically, students are asked to interrupt this structured cycle and to engage in "process days" where they reflect on the overall objectives of the course and on the nature of the process and content of the course. This process assists students' learning by reducing ambiguity and keeping them focused on the topic at hand. It further reduces the anxiety that can be associated with engaging each other in unfamiliar territory. Finally, students are learning that discussions and debates, that at one time were politically charged, can become intellectual exchanges that have purpose and meaning.

Ground Rules That Enhance Comfort and Voice

Among large research universities, the Center for Teaching and Learning at the University of North Carolina-Chapel Hill has provided an excellent set of resources to faculty on teaching for inclusion. While inclusion can incorporate a variety of topics (course content, learning outcomes, teaching styles, etc.), a discussion about the student "voice" should focus on the degree to which:

- Students may feel alienated by classroom discussions.
- Students feel distressed because some aspects of the course threatens their identity.
- Students voice criticisms of other students and/or the instructor.
- Students are uncharacteristically quiet.
- Students feel that anyone will say anything at any time.
- Only certain students have the right to speak about certain issues.
- Misinformation exists, and students are responsible for learning about such misinformation instead of perpetuating it.

The UNC Center for Teaching and Learning (CTL) suggests that one way instructors can create a comfort zone for students is to lay out the ground rules for discussing emotionally charged, controversial, and potentially offensive topics. It is also suggested, and this is very important, that the ground rules will help only if the course objective and the instructors' personality and teaching style are compatible with such explicit rules. For example, a passive-aggressive personality would undermine the instructor's goal of consistency in applying ground rules. An instructor who uses only an analytical teaching style may not be able to elicit and affirm the "affective" response that indicates that a student is engaged in learning.

Among the guidelines that the CTL offers for structured classroom discussions are:

- Everyone in class has both a right and an obligation to participate in discussions and, if called upon, should try to respond.
- Always listen carefully and with an open mind to the contributions of others.
- Ask for clarification when you don't understand a point someone has made.
- If you challenge others' ideas, do so with factual evidence and appropriate logic.
- If others challenge your ideas, be willing to change your mind if they demonstrate errors in your logic or your use of the facts.
- Don't introduce irrelevant issues into the discussion.
- If others have made a point with which you agree, don't repeat it (unless you have something important to add).
- Be efficient in your discourse, make your points, and then yield to others.

- Above all, avoid ridicule and try to respect the beliefs of others, even if those beliefs differ from yours (The Guided Discussion, 1992, For Your Consideration, p. 12)

Another example of support that can assist faculty with issues of inclusion in the college classroom is from the Derek Bok Center for Teaching and Learning at Harvard University. The Center sponsors a Tip Sheet that empowers the user to create the conditions under which diversity can flourish. While reiterating comments that are made frequently, the Tip Sheet is valuable because of its use of topical categories under which various strategies are enumerated.

For example, under the heading, "Activate student voices," two of the listed suggestions include:

- When appropriate, create opportunities for students to personalize course content with examples from their own reality or history so they can make connections between ideas learned in the classroom and those learned through life experiences.
- Make it safe for everyone to voice his or her views by accepting all views as worthy of consideration. Don't permit scapegoating of any student or any view, and don't leave students out on a limb.

Under the heading, "Devise personal strategies in advance for managing yourself and the class," one important suggestion is: Try to anticipate what topics may be explosive and design pedagogical strategies (small groups, writing that expresses students' attitudes and emotions, and reflection responses) that may assist in managing sensitive topics.

Under the heading, "Interrupt blatantly racist and discriminatory behaviors when they emerge in class," an important suggestion is: Try not to let yourself be rattled by the event, or at least try not to let it look as if you are rattled. If you as the teacher can hold yourself steady, you will create an environment in which people can work out the issues that arise.

Finally, under the heading, "Turn potentially hot moments into powerful learning experiences," an important suggestion is: Use the passion and arguments to look at how group dynamics work—who speaks and who does not, who allies him or herself with whom, who plays what role—and to think about how the group wants to work. Many faculty could benefit from such resource information, especially when it is pedagogically sound, as in the case of the Bok Center. Faculty should establish venues for periodic discourse about inclusion and their discipline with the goal of documenting the results of a scholarly forum.

The ultimate expectations of the academy in terms of facilitating student voice are associated with outcomes rather than process. However, the choice of process or strategies must be rooted in what we know works, or in well-reasoned and evidenced-based ideas about what can work. The fundamental structure can be simple, but the devil is in the details.

In developing a first-year vehicle for engagement, a college or university can begin with (a) something students value highly (religion); (b) something of which students are aware, to varying degrees (political and social crises); (c) a structure that supports the autonomy and anonymity of cognitive deliberations; (d) stated learning outcomes that encourage vocal expression, levels of questioning, self-confidence, and course content; and (e) a reflective linkage among readings, class exercises, and curricular content. A comprehensive and instructional example of how conceptual frameworks and pedagogical practices can translate into meaningful outcomes is found in *Teaching for Diversity and Social Justice* (Adams, Bell, & Griffin, 2007). This volume represents more than 30 years of collaboration among faculty and graduate and undergraduate students, who address a number of topics linked by the themes of oppression and social justice (racism, White privilege, immigration, sexism, heterosexism, transgender oppression, religious oppression, anti-Jewish oppression and anti-Semitism, classism, ableism, and adultism). The book covers extensive curriculum designs that are both practical and pedagogically sound, interactive experiences for students and facilitators that promote thoughtful engagement and inquiry and thoroughly updated resources, references, and examples, including a CD-ROM.

One could argue that the challenges that emerge when one confronts oppressive assumptions, beliefs, and behaviors such as those mentioned above would disrupt the learning process in an academic setting. The chapters in this volume overcome this potential obstacle by setting goals for learning that make sense educationally, by using a coherent curriculum, and by meeting students where they are, and then building on their questions and concerns. Bell and Griffin (2007) developed some of the following design considerations of teaching social justice education courses (pp. 67–68):

- Identify relevant characteristics of participants and develop goals appropriate to the learning needs of the group.
- Match the environment to student social-emotional learning processes so the environment supports them appropriately at different points in the course.
- Select specific class activities to address key concepts in social justice education and match these to student needs.
- Accommodate a variety of learning styles.
- Be flexible and ready to make design changes as needed while a class is in progress.
- Evaluate the course and grade student performance: identify different components of evaluation as a key part of course design.

Throughout the chapters the authors seek to sequence and scaffold the course design and goals to accomplish an accepted best practice, to adjust teaching to the needs of the learners, and to promote intentional gains in their cognitive complexity.

Institutions often wrestle with the topical choices they make to ease students into a purposeful and productive critical discourse. For example, some academic leaders are more willing than others to ask first-year students to address such religious issues and questions as: What is the role of religion in sustaining activism on behalf of racial and gender equality and combating injustice? Compare and contrast the strategies used by Osama bin Laden and Dr. Martin Luther King Jr. in their approaches to religion and social activism. What social issues have the most potential to produce interfaith cooperation? Why do many students, who voice public support for their religious faith, remain silent about the political or social inequities they recognize? Can an institution's beliefs and values about its own mission, culture, and/ or tradition silence students' voices by making them fear retaliation or being "outed"?

The Power of Student Journals

As a tribute to the increasing diversity of its physical location and the student population it serves, the University of California, Los Angeles, sponsors a number of student journals. One in particular has its home in the Academic Advancement Program (AAP), an academic support program for diverse students. The journal, *Crossing Borders*, reflects the aspirations, struggles, challenges, and triumphs of AAP students and their families.

The student editors and contributors are members of Chicano/a studies classes taught by Professor Aldolfo Bermeo. Thus, the journal reflects academic content and expertise as well as an ethnographic voice that is centered in cultural and historical reality. This notion of ethnic centeredness, rather than the floating reality of participating in the dominant culture, is captured in one of the journal narratives by Martha A. Rivas: "The RIVAS Experience: Revolucionando, the Imposed Immigrant Identity via Academic Success."

Not new to the academic experience of undergraduates, student journals have been associated with multiple purposes (writing, reflection, identity development, etc.). Ethnographic journals represent powerful dimensions of student voices, and their value is enhanced when guided by a framework that can evoke the essence of meaning for the writer and a diversity of audiences.

A Technological Tool to Encourage Student Voice

Do online discussions involving anonymous communicators enable more honest dialogue on sensitive topics related to diversity? That is one of the questions that a number of faculty are studying at Pepperdine University as it pertains to externally and internally funded diversity efforts. Gambill (2003, p. 15) describes how the university, since 1994, has used the Digital Portfolio Assessment Project (DPAP) to conduct qualitative, longitudinal studies of cognitive and affective student learning and development. One four-year study, entitled DPAP 2005, examines the transformation of students' cultural perspectives in response to the various ways diversity is embedded in curricular and cocurricular contexts.

While the value of student portfolios has been well established, they require conscientious attention, authenticity, and a great deal of motivation on the part of the student. DPAP 2005 requires students to submit journal entries online in response to writing prompts and participating in yearly focus groups. When students respond in real time to online cues, their tendency to provide authentic responses is enhanced. The *immixJournal* serves as a password-protected Web site that encourages student interaction because students can read and respond to each other's journal entries.

Twenty-first-century college students generally are moderately technologically savvy, so they tend to be less anxious when they communicate in cyberspace. In other words they may be more willing to share their voice in an online discourse community. DPAP 2005 allows students to adopt aliases as their identity. Moreover, if they choose, students can participate in face-to-face or virtual roundtable focus groups. Online assessment of the student voice tends to be enriched and easily captured as longitudinal data since it is written. The technological challenges of establishing communities of discourse in cyberspace are eased because of the level of sophistication that most campuses have already established in administrative, academic, and student data computing.

In this discussion of facilitators and inhibitors of student voice, we cannot lose sight of or devalue the relationship of "voice" to our fundamental outcomes associated with student learning and development. Student voices are expressed in a cultural, historical, political, and temporal context that must be linked to the goals and objectives of the college or university's educational context.

References

Adams, M., Bell, L. A., & Griffin, P. (2007). *Teaching for diversity and social justice.* New York: Routledge.

Bell, L. A., & Griffin, P. (2007). Designing social justice education courses. In M. Adams (Ed.), *Teaching for diversity and social justice* (pp. 67–87). New York: Routledge.

Bennett, J. M., & Bennett, M. J. (2004). Developing intercultural sensitivity: An integrative approach to global and domestic diversity. In D. Landis, J. M. Bennett, & M. J. Bennett (Eds.), *Handbook of intercultural training* (3rd ed.), pp. 147–165. Thousand Oaks, CA: Sage.

Cioffi, F. L. (2005, May 20). Argumentation in a culture of discord. *The Chronicle of Higher Education*, pp. B6–8.

Gambill, H. (2003). The Digital Portfolio Assessment Project 2005: Using the on-line *immixJournal* to qualitatively assess the campus climate's fostering of diversity. *Diversity Digest, 7*(4), 15.

Garcia-Preto, N. (1982). Puerto Rican families. In M. McGoldrick, J. Giordano, & J. K. Pierce (Eds.), *Ethnicity and family therapy* (pp. 164–186). New York: Guilford Press.

Guided Discussion, The. (1992, February). For Your Consideration, 12. Retrieved from http://ctl.unc.edu/fyc12.html

Jalomo, R. E., & Rendon, L. I. (2004). Moving to a new culture: The upside and downside of the transition to college. In L. I. Rendon, M. Garcia, & D. Person (Eds.), *Transforming the first year of college for students of color* (pp. 37–52). Columbia: University of South Carolina.

Kobasa, S. C. (1979). Stressful life events, personality and health: An inquiry into hardiness. *Journal of Personality and Social Psychology, 37*, 1–11.

LeSure-Lester, G. E., & King, N. (2005). Racial-ethnic divergences in social anxiety among college students. *Journal of College Student Retention, 6*(3), 359–367.

Lifton, D. E., Seay, S., & Bushko, A. (2004). Measuring undergraduate hardiness as an indicator of persistence to graduation within four years. In L. M. Duranczyk, J. L. Higbee, & D. B. Lundell (Eds.), *Best practices for access and retention in higher education* (pp. 103–113). Minneapolis: University of Minnesota.

Mooney, K. M., Fordham, T., & Lehr, V. D. (2005). A faculty development program to promote engaged classroom dialogue: The Oral Communication Institute. In S. Chadwick-Blossey & D. Robertson (Eds.), *To improve the academy: Resources for faculty, instructional, and organizational development* (vol. 23, pp. 220–235). San Francisco: Jossey Bass (originally published by Anker Publishing).

Okazaki, S. (1997). Sources of ethnic differences between Asian American and White American college students on measures of depression and social anxiety. *Journal of Abnormal Psychology, 106*, 52–60.

Osei-Kofi, N., Richards, S. L., & Smith, D. G. (2004). Inclusion, reflection, and the politics of knowledge: On working toward the realization of inclusive classroom environments. In L. I. Rendon, M. Garcia, & D. Person (Eds.), *Transforming the first year of college students of color* (pp. 55–66). Columbia: University of South Carolina.

Pavela, G. (2006, December 1). Only speech codes should be censored. *The Chronicle of Higher Education*, pp. B8–9.

Pond, S. B. (2004). All in balance: Psychology 201 "Controversial issues in psychology." In V. Lee (Ed.), *Teaching and learning through inquiry* (pp. 31–40). Sterling, VA: Stylus.

Rendon, L. I. (1994). Validating culturally diverse students: Toward a new model of learning and student development. *Innovative Higher Education, 19*, 33–51.

Rendon, L. I., Garcia, M., & Person, D. (Eds.). (2004). *Transforming the first-year experience for students of color*. Monograph No. 38. Columbia: University of South Carolina, National Resource Center for the First-Year Experience and Students in Transition.

Rodgers, C. R. (2006). Attending to student voice: The impact of descriptive feedback on learning and teaching. *Curriculum Inquiry, 36*(2), 209–237.

Schlenker, B. R., & Leary, M. R. (1982). Social anxiety and self-presentation: A conceptualization and model. *Psychological Bulletin, 92*, 641–669.

Siefert, K., & Butler, I. (1993). Multicultural teaching in public health: A course on gender, race, ethnicity, and health. In D. Schoem, L. Frankel, X. Zuniga, & E. Lewis (Eds.), *Multicultural teaching in the university* (pp. 110–118). Westport, CT: Praeger.

Tannen, D. (1998). *The argument culture: Moving from debate to dialogue.* New York: Random House.

White, J. (1991). *Toward a Black psychology.* Berkeley, CA: Cobb & Henry.

8

RESPONSIBILITY AND
ACCOUNTABILITY

A Willingness to Examine Our Promises and Processes

I have attempted to characterize incorporating diversity and globalism activities and outcomes into the traditional teaching and learning paradigm as a natural and necessary fit. Moreover, I have argued that the educational concepts of quality and excellence cannot be fully realized or thought of in a 21st-century context without authentically addressing both outcomes. Those who claim a perceived threat (lowered standards, political correctness) to institutional quality and reputation are only trying to generate anxieties that are misplaced and to maintain the status quo. The notion of "dumbing down" can apply when students are not given the tools to expand their knowledge base, engage new and different perspectives, accept the changing nature of the world, and understand that intellectual diversity and globalism equalize the value of shared experiences. Institutional leaders who reject this position are abdicating the responsibility that underscores their core mission and their often-repeated statements about access, success, excellence, scholarship, and student preparation for the 21st century. The clarion calls for such outcomes come from leaders in virtually every organizational setting. For example, a comprehensive report, released in 2005 by the bipartisan Abraham Lincoln Commission on Study Abroad and titled, "Global Competence and National Needs: One Million Students Studying Abroad" (see www.nafsa.org/public_policy.sec/public_policy_document/study-abroad_ 1/lincoln_commission_report), argues for a significant increase in the number of college students who study overseas to help them develop a global perspective and a better understanding of the world outside U.S. borders.

The report also emphasizes the need to involve more diverse and nontraditional students in study-abroad activities.

As Figure 8.1 indicates, evaluation of teaching becomes significantly more robust when evaluation of diversity and globalism are linked to the more generic evaluation of teaching. In developing the questionnaire in Figure 8.1, I have attempted to keep the focus on teaching and learning outcomes and the processes associated with them.

The efficacy of this type of survey instrument presupposes that early in a course the instructor discusses with the class the goals and outcomes of the course and provides recurring examples of when these goals and outcomes occur and why they are valuable. Certain concepts, such as inquiry-guided learning, need to be defined for students and understood as part of active learning strategies. For many students this approach may represent the first time they have been asked to link course content to actual teaching and learning outcomes and to grasp the symbiotic roles of instructor and learner. The additional challenge is to place these outcomes in the context of diversity and globalism.

Latragna and Anderson (2003) developed a survey instrument to assess students' perceptions of overall classroom dynamics in a given course while also exploring diversity considerations. In fact, the researchers hoped that embedding questions about diversity and multiculturalism within the broader context of classroom issues would result in a more valid set of student responses. A pilot survey involved more than 5,000 respondents across four institutional types (community college, historically Black, comprehensive, and research I) to establish content validity and interitem reliability.

A 36-item survey (including one additional open-ended question) included four general categories and two related specifically to diversity. The general ones were (1) student-student interactions; (2) student-faculty interactions; (3) learning styles; and (4) student preference to work alone or in groups. The diversity categories were (1) classroom climate for different groups and (2) an inclusive curriculum. Students' responses per item were recorded on a five-item Likert scale (strongly agree . . . strongly disagree) or a sixth choice of not applicable.

The survey also collected demographic information (sex, age, race/ethnicity, disability), grade-point average, semesters in college, and academic program. Post-administration focus groups during the pilot revealed that students did not perceive the survey to be a diversity survey. A strong information base comprised of students' varied perceptions of classroom climate can become a

FIGURE 8.1
Ratings for Reaching Effectiveness

(Scale: 1 = strongly disagree . . . 5 = strongly agree)

The instructor of this course:

1. Can effectively communicate his or her knowledge about the traditional course content to students.
2. Can effectively communicate his or her knowledge about inclusive and non-traditional course content to students.
3. Treats all students in the course equitably and with respect.
4. Can verbalize ideas and thought processes so that they are relevant to the differing experiences of students.
5. Provides a comfortable and effective learning environment.
6. Manages conflict or difficult dialogues effectively.
7. Challenges students intellectually.
8. Provides the appropriate tools to help students engage and benefit from intellectual diversity and globalism.
9. Promotes thinking by asking students different types of questions.
10. Provides opportunities for students to generate their own questions.
11. Gives students the opportunity to benefit from the diversity of other learners.
12. Uses creative and innovative assignments and activities.
13. Incorporates contemporary issues and controversial topics into the learning experience in effective ways.
14. Motivates students to have an enthusiasm for learning.
15. Provides opportunities for students to evaluate their own strengths and weaknesses as learners.
16. Provides opportunities for students to evaluate the work and contributions of other students.
17. Varies teaching techniques to facilitate learning.
18. Varies teaching techniques to facilitate intellectual diversity and globalism.
19. Uses different instructional techniques to support diverse learning styles.
20. Encourages students to share their cultural backgrounds and experiences.
21. Enables students to feel comfortable expressing their "voice" in class.
22. Helps students to understand why intellectual diversity and globalism are important in their major.
23. Helps students to understand why intellectual diversity and globalism are important aspects of liberal learning.
24. Allows students to incorporate inquiry-guided learning at a comfortable pace.
25. Encourages students to take responsibility for developing their own learning community.

partial indicator of a definition of teaching effectiveness and ultimately under-graduate excellence. The entire survey is found in Appendix D.

Jon Rust, a professor of textile engineering at North Carolina State University, uses a senior design capstone course (TE 402) as a laboratory to address diversity, tolerance, and globalism in the context of more traditional course-based outcomes. Students in the course engage in experiential exercises and then evaluate those experiences using a cross-cultural experience rubric (a set of criteria and a scoring scale used to assess and evaluate students' work). Students can use the rubric to develop, revise, and judge their own work. Professor Rust uses a series of layered questions as the rubric in the capstone course:

Cross-Cultural Experience Rubric

Why are these questions useful?
1. Why did you choose this event?
   • Potentially uncomfortable; expressed curiosity; preconceived ideas about those involved
2. What experiences were rejected or avoided. Why?
   • Willingness to acknowledge what was rejected
   • Willingness to explore rejection: beliefs, fears, expectations
   • Willingness to explore where beliefs and fears originate
3. How did you feel being there? (+ experience versus expected)
   • Observations of feelings (e.g., fears, doubts, surprises, etc.), resulting actions, anticipations, comparisons, challenges
4. How was experience different from that of your own culture?
5. How might that difference contribute to society?
   • Provide different views, ways of understanding, enrich culture, expand human experience, learning, and growth
6. What did you learn about yourself?
   • Previous stereotypes and expectations altered
   • What privileges (or lack thereof) can you identify as a member of your own cultural group?
   • What had you feared; was that fear justified?
   • How your and others' behaviors alter in different environments with different groups
   • Anticipations versus actual experience
   • How your upbringing contributed to previously held beliefs

Such an innovative (and to some instructors—risky) approach to embedding diversity must address fundamental questions about merging course grading and program assessment techniques. Can this assignment be used to demonstrate that students are meeting program outcomes? Can the rubric be used to grade students? What changes are needed to make the rubric a grading instrument in addition to an assessment instrument?

Including cross-cultural experiences does not detract from the traditional outcomes associated with a capstone course in textile engineering; rather, it provides an added outcome that enhances the real-world application of the overall course content. For example, evidence is now available demonstrating that TE graduates possess and use the personal and professional skills necessary to function effectively in a team; appreciate and respect cultural and socioeconomic diversity; demonstrate excellent communication skills across contexts and groups; and recognize the value of contributions of and work effectively with team members from different disciplines. For the students in TE 402, the immersion experience, coupled with the course work, underscores the relationship between the theoretical and practical, the academic realm and the real world.

Global Learning

Hovland (2005, p. 1) identifies two components that describe global learning: (1) successful preparation of students to live responsible, productive, and creative lives in a dramatically changing world, and (2) shaping students' identities as they are shaped by such factors as power and privilege, within both a multicultural U.S. democracy and an interconnected and unequal world. Global learning can refer to long-term developmental preparation that depends on an enhanced knowledge base, and it can simultaneously encompass a psychocultural dimension that is both personal and experiential. At the most fundamental level, however, global learning results from successful attainment of learning outcomes, especially those enabling students to become reflective and analytical learners. Thus, global learning shares common goals with interdisciplinary learning, liberal education, a general education or core curriculum experience, scientific learning, and learning in a capstone course.

While global learning and diversity education can represent pathways to similar learning goals for our students, their interconnectedness remains a distant and unattainable goal for many campuses. Institutional leaders must examine the nature and source of this educational vacuum. Again, we can return to previous chapters: Is the problem structural (marginalized groups and locations)? Is the problem conceptual (the dominance of a Eurocentric ideology)? Is the problem curricular (an ineffective or nonexistent revision of the general education curriculum)? Is the problem political (backlash from conservative groups)? Is the problem resource-related (no new faculty positions are available to hire experts in globalism and diversity)? Is the problem pedagogical (globalism and diversity are not translated into teaching and learning outcomes)?

Platforms and Pathways to Infusion

Global learning and education can be viewed along a continuum with generic program outcomes at one end, more sophisticated program and learning outcomes somewhere in the middle, and a well-developed degree program that creates "globally literate" students at the other end. For those institutions seeking to infuse global perspectives into the curriculum content or into instructional goals, a decision must be made about the framework that will best support this decision. For example, internships and experiential learning opportunities can be created that emphasize global activities, or students can undertake in their senior year a capstone project that summarizes the impact of a global curricular track. Global outcomes can be embedded within General Education or core curriculum outcomes, within religious literacy outcomes, as part of writing across curriculum outcomes, or into liberal learning outcomes that are associated with the principles of democracy and citizenship. In terms of student learning objectives, globalism can be represented as cognitive competencies, cultural competencies and skills, values and personal choices, communicative competencies, interdisciplinary connections, or workplace competencies. The above iterations may or may not occur in a phase development model that moves students from a seminal or introductory phase to a more reflective or integrative position. If a phased approach is not used, how do students advance to actual competencies?

My purpose in outlining what is clearly not an exhaustive list of pathways to global learning is twofold: (1) to recognize the varied and sometimes complex options that await campus leaders, and (2) to suggest that the incorporation of global learning should not take precedence over defining what it is and why we want it to occur. If our goal is to develop habits of mind in students, we must first define what we think that means and how it should look as an end product—that, in turn, should guide our selection of the structural pathway.

Centers of Responsibility

A powerful publication has emerged from the joint efforts of two higher education organizations that offers a reflective process to institutional leaders as they seek to address the personal and operational commitments that must be present to link diversity to mission-driven change. *Now Is the Time: Meeting the Challenge for a Diverse Academy* (American Association of State Colleges and Universities [AASCU]/National Association of State Universities and Land-Grant Colleges [NASULGC], 2005, p. 24) uses a conceptual framework, called "Centers of Responsibility for Diversity," for facilitating campuswide conversations across all levels of institutional functioning. The centers are composed of reflective questions, a structured discussion process and a facilitator's guide, based on four important assumptions:

- Intentional and thoughtful planning is required if higher education in the United States is to integrate diversity into all facets of our institutional mission and practice.
- Leadership competence needs to be constructed. Participation in the process is as significant a goal as developing measurable outcomes for change.
- Leaders need a safe place to explore issues and create change. While potential conflict may accompany difficult diversity discussions, leaders can provide climates for discussion that allow students to explore challenges and propose innovative solutions.
- Leaders must model desired practice to align support across campus.

The 11 centers include a series of questions organized around six themes: recruitment, retention, partnerships, campus climate, professional development, and assessment. The centers reflect the organizational structure that is common to most colleges and universities: academic affairs, student affairs, business and finance, athletics, development and university relations, governing boards, presidents/chancellors, faculty, staff, students, and student leadership.

The leaders of each area and the group participants respond to the reflective questions as individuals first and then as part of their respective unit, department, program, or division. Certain questions may be addressed across several institutional areas because of their broad significance. For example, "What have I/we done to support the academic success of diverse students?" pertains to academic affairs, student affairs, athletics, faculty, and certain staff.

Asking reflective questions represents one component of a process, but individuals and groups also need a way to evaluate performance. The centers are able to use a measurement tool, the Diversity Assessment Scale, that allows participants to assign a rating number to their responses on a five-point Likert scale (resisting = 1, separating = 2, assimilating = 3, integrating = 4, transforming = 5).

The overall design of the centers and the campus-wide process, including its scope and time frame, is determined by the president or chancellor, who works closely with the designated administrative coordinator, who actually oversees the process. This position is very important to the success of the initiative since the administrative coordinator monitors the process to ensure full engagement by all participants. Among this person's most targeted responsibilities are:

- advance preparation that promotes a shared background of understanding;
- framing the conversation for participants;
- establishing ground rules for communication;
- creating and facilitating group interaction;
- engaging in reflective discussion;
- defining goals, commitments, and accountability;
- reviewing and summarizing feedback; and
- conduct a closing activity.

The conceptualization of "Centers of Responsibility" finds precedent in organizational theories that differentiate among types of learning that do or do not produce transformative change. Argyris and Schon (1996) identify single-loop learning as looking outward (by individuals or institutions) to find structural or programmatic solutions to problems. Double-loop learning entails the ability to reflect on a problem from within and then to rethink one's own values, beliefs, and practices. Pena, Bensimon, and Colyar (2006) have formalized an institutional change intervention known as Equity for All that uses progressively more complex and intense phases. The core reflective activity, which involves defining a problem within a specified context, consists of three elements: situated inquiry, practitioner-as-researcher, and community practice. When drawn to an appropriate conclusion, the community of practice is equivalent to a Center of Responsibility.

The incentive to engage in reflection correlates highly with the willingness to analyze oneself introspectively. The questions that prompt engagement of issues, problems, and solutions must draw individuals and the institution into a critical dialogue. Several years ago I proposed the following questions to an audience at an American Dental Association conference:

- What are the academic components of a health care model that trains and educates quality professionals who are drawn from diverse populations? To what degree does your institution reflect such a model?
- Are we using the most effective collaborations (internally and externally) that create and reinforce a pipeline of prospective diverse students?
- Do our admission criteria and decisions account for ethnic and cultural concerns? Do they account for changing national demographics?
- How do the teaching activities/goals of professional school faculty reflect a commitment to diversity?
- Have we allocated sufficient resources to support the needs of underrepresented students and faculty? How have we responded to the questions/criticisms of research faculty?
- In our clinical training, do we emphasize how the belief systems of diverse clients affect their perceptions of service delivery?
- In the diversity discussion, what factors affect the level of client cooperation and compliance with a prescribed treatment program?
- Do we know if faculty beliefs about service delivery to diverse clients foster negative images and feelings among students?

While I did not offer a structured process to accompany this line of questioning, my goal was to initiate a critical examination of how professional schools address the challenges associated with diversity. It is surprising that, of the 200 or so presentations listed in the conference program, only one other addressed any aspect of diversity.

Many campuses have attempted to construct an effective framework to engage various individuals and groups in a critical discourse about diversity, but for various reasons their success has been limited. The adaptive strengths of the "centers" model are threefold: (1) responsibility and accountability are conjoined in concrete and meaningful ways; (2) a structured process is used that is comprehensive in scope; and (3) engagement results from reflective questioning and purposeful dialogue. The joint efforts of the American Association of State Colleges and Universities (AASCU) and the National Association of State Universities and Land-Grant Colleges (NASULGC) have produced an invaluable tool that should be examined closely by institutional leaders who exhibit the courage to transform the culture of their campuses.

Final Thoughts

To move toward the suggestions and recommendations contained in this book will require thoughtful preparation, visible leadership, renewed aspirations, and the firm belief that diversity and globalism benefit all students and the entire faculty community. Inclusive excellence elevates the traditional definition of excellence to one that enhances meaning, moral value, and social significance. At each of our campuses, our gains and our successes should become part of the public domain of shared practice until the rich array of initiatives evolves into a blinding mosaic. Higher education is one of the few remaining areas where such a profound outcome can occur.

Our charge is to build and support the platforms and pathways that embed diversity and globalism within the academy, and to commit to developing an intellectual community of educators, students, and administrators that expands the boundaries of our campuses into a world where all members can benefit from our expertise and passion.

References

American Associaton of State Colleges and Universities (AASCU)/National Association of State Universities and Land-Grant Colleges (NASULGC) Task Force on

Diversity. (2005). *Now is the time: Meeting the challenge for a diverse academy.* Washington, DC : Authors.

Argyris, C., & Schon, D. (1996). *Organizational learning II: Theory, method and practice.* Reading, MA: Addison Wesley.

Hovland, K. (2005). Shared futures: Global learning and social responsibility. Diversity Digest, 8(3), 1, 16–17.

Latragna, P., & Anderson, J. (2003). Student survey on classroom environment (for information, e-mail jaanderson@uamail.albany.edu).

Pena, E. V., Bensimon, E. M., & Colyar, J. (2006). Contextual problem defining: Learning to think and act from the standpoint of equity. *Liberal Education, 92*(2), 48–55.

Summary of Findings in Relation to Research Questions

What **discourses** are used?	How are **problems** represented?	How are **solutions** represented?	What are predominant **images**?
Discourse of Access	• Significant barriers to entrance to and advancement in the university • Discriminatory practices • Obstacles to full participation	• Increase the presence and prevalence of diverse individuals • Remove obstacles and barriers • Redress inequities	*Outsider* "excluded" "marginalized" "underrepresented" "unwelcome" "hardly noticeable"
Discourse of Entrée	• Poor selection processes • Ineffective and inequitable recruitment practices and processes • Untrained search committees • Limited pool of candidates and difficulty attracting diverse persons • Inadequate compensation and benefits • Inaccessible facilities	• Improve recruitment and selection processes (e.g., advertising, marketing, strategic hiring) • Improve search committees • Identify diverse pools (e.g., precollege programs, partnerships with MSIs • Strategic use of funding (e.g., scholarships, wages) • Accessible facilities	"inaccessible" "lack of applicants" "difficulty attracting minorities" "relatively few" "inability to recruit and hire minorities" "excluded or routinely limited" "eliminate barriers and obstacles" "feed the pipeline"

What **discourses** are used?	How are **problems** represented?	How are **solutions** represented?	What are predominant **images**?
Discourse of Representation	• Inadequate representation, supported with quantifiable data • Poor recruitment; • attrition • Slow to no advancement • Gaps in curriculum	• Increase numbers, especially leadership • Improve retention (e.g., through mentoring, professional development) • Revise policies • "Infuse diversity into the curriculum"	"women are not well represented" "women and minorities are underrepresented" "remain hardly noticeable" "increase prevalence" "widen the net"
Discourse of Affirmation	• "Chilly" climate • Exclusionary messages and symbols (e.g., mascot, traditions, segregated past)	• Profess institutional commitment to diversity • Create recognition and awards ceremonies and host cultural celebrations • Develop resource office • Deliver education and training • Conduct climate surveys	"(un)welcome" "(under)valued" "(un)appreciated" "(dis)respect" "celebrate" "recognize" "honor" "exclude"/ "include"

What **discourses** are used?	How are **problems** represented?	How are **solutions** represented?	What are predominant **images**?
Discourse of Disadvantage	• Educational failure • Nonpromotion, no advancement, no tenure • Inadequate and unequal compensation and benefits	• Offer summer programs to compensate for deficiencies • Professional development • Create mentoring programs • Offer financial aid, scholarships • Ensure salary equity	*At-risk* "economically disadvantaged" "academically underprepared" "needy"
Discourse of Discrimination	• Isolation and oppression • Historic and contemporary discrimination • Hate crimes • Harassment • Bias • Unfair treatment	• Eliminate unfair practices and policies • Offer support services (e.g., ombudsman) • Deliver training and education • Facilitate intergroup dialogue	*Victim* "unsafe" "abused" "silenced" "insulted" "harassed" "targeted groups" "discriminated against" "threatened"
Marketplace Discourse	• Inability to compete • Unprepared to respond to "changing market conditions" • Scarce resources and declining public support	• Develop diversity programs with market value • Strategic use of funding	*Commodity* "capitalize on . . . increasing diversity" "take full advantage . . . of diversity" "make effective use of diversity" "as important . . . as technology"

What **discourses** are used?	How are **problems** represented?	How are **solutions** represented?	What are predominant **images**?
Discourse of Excellence	• Overemphasis on diversity could compromise institutional excellence	• Establish and promote reputation • Develop performance indicators to measure success • Benchmarking	"world-class distinction" "prominence" "high-quality" "prestige" "first-class" "high standards" "exceptional" minorities
Discourse of Managerialism	• Poor management or lack of leadership • Insufficient accountability • Absence of coordinated efforts • Inadequate progress on or achievement of diversity goals	• Efficient management • Enhance coordination • Improve processes, procedures, and practices • Routinization of assessment and evaluation • Establish mechanisms for quality assurance • Ensure accountability	"efficiency" "productivity" "accountability" "coordination" "managing and leveraging diversity" "effective utilization" of diversity
Discourse of Democracy	• Inequality • Historical and contemporary inequities • Failure to be inclusive	• Facilitate open, public dialogue and participatory decision making (e.g., town meetings, presidential commissions)	*Change agent* "right thing to do" "alliance" "solidarity" "collaborative spirit" "grassroots action"

Perceptions of Academic Leadership and Competency and Diversity Outcomes

Your responses reflect your evaluation of which of the following offices? (Check only one.)

____ Provost and/or VP for Academic Affairs

____ Vice Provost or Associate Provost/VP for Academic Affairs

____ Vice President for Instruction

____ Academic Dean

____ Associate Academic Dean

____ Department Chair or Head

____ Academic Affairs Officer (Diversity, Enrollment Management, Assessment, Institutional Research)

For *each* statement below, place an "x" on each of the two scales (leadership and competency). Your response should reflect your evaluation of actual behaviors, not your perception of a person's potential.

- Leadership is defined by activities such as framing issues, charting direction, articulating goals, developing a consensus, and projecting a leadership presence.
- Competency refers to the knowledge and expertise that one exhibits in advancing goals and objectives to achieve some valued outcome.

1. Communicates the importance and value of linking diversity and globalism to academic excellence and the mission of his or her office.

Leadership	_____	_____	_____	_____	_____
	Exhibits No Evidence		Exhibits Moderate Evidence		Exhibits Significant Evidence

Competency	_____	_____	_____	_____	_____
	Exhibits No Evidence		Exhibits Moderate Evidence		Exhibits Significant Evidence

2. Contributes to the development and implementation of a comprehensive campus-wide diversity plan.

Leadership _____ _____   _____ _____   _____ _____

       Exhibits No   Exhibits   Exhibits   Not

       Evidence   Moderate   Significant   Applicable

                                  Evidence   Evidence

Competency _____ _____   _____ _____   _____ _____

       Exhibits No   Exhibits   Exhibits   Not

       Evidence   Moderate   Significant   Applicable

                                  Evidence   Evidence

3. Closely monitors the campus climate as it is experienced by underrepresented groups.

Leadership _____ _____   _____ _____   _____

       Exhibits No   Exhibits   Exhibits

       Evidence   Moderate   Significant

                                  Evidence   Evidence

Competency _____ _____   _____ _____   _____

       Exhibits No   Exhibits   Exhibits

       Evidence   Moderate   Significant

                                  Evidence   Evidence

4. Conducts substantive evaluations of personnel that include specific criteria on diversity efforts and achievements.

Leadership _____ _____   _____ _____   _____

       Exhibits No   Exhibits   Exhibits

       Evidence   Moderate   Significant

                                  Evidence   Evidence

Competency _____ _____   _____ _____   _____

       Exhibits No   Exhibits   Exhibits

       Evidence   Moderate   Significant

                                  Evidence   Evidence

5. Engages faculty in critical conversations about diversity and globalism in relation to pedagogy, classroom inclusion, and/or curricular transformation.

Leadership _____ _____   _____ _____   _____

       Exhibits No   Exhibits   Exhibits

       Evidence   Moderate   Significant

                                  Evidence   Evidence

Competency _____ _____   _____ _____   _____

       Exhibits No   Exhibits   Exhibits

       Evidence   Moderate   Significant

                                  Evidence   Evidence

6. Understands the diversity issues that are associated with an open-admissions institution (two- and four-year institutions only).

Leadership _____ _____   Exhibits _____   Exhibits _____   Not
           Exhibits No   Moderate   Significant   Applicable
           Evidence   Evidence   Evidence

Competency _____ _____   Exhibits _____   Exhibits _____   Not
           Exhibits No   Moderate   Significant   Applicable
           Evidence   Evidence   Evidence

7. Clearly articulates the relationship between institutional change and diversity.

Leadership _____ _____   Exhibits _____   Exhibits _____
           Exhibits No   Moderate   Significant
           Evidence   Evidence   Evidence

Competency _____ _____   Exhibits _____   Exhibits _____
           Exhibits No   Moderate   Significant
           Evidence   Evidence   Evidence

8. Integrates a focus on diversity and/or globalism within the traditional roles of his or her position.

Leadership _____ _____   Exhibits _____   Exhibits _____
           Exhibits No   Moderate   Significant
           Evidence   Evidence   Evidence

Competency _____ _____   Exhibits _____   Exhibits _____
           Exhibits No   Moderate   Significant
           Evidence   Evidence   Evidence

9. Involves diverse faculty, staff and/or students in the critical decision making associated with his or her office.

Leadership _____ _____   Exhibits _____   Exhibits _____
           Exhibits No   Moderate   Significant
           Evidence   Evidence   Evidence

Competency _____ _____   Exhibits _____   Exhibits _____
           Exhibits No   Moderate   Significant
           Evidence   Evidence   Evidence

10. Raises the level of sophistication about the critical discourse on diversity and globalism associated with his or her area of responsibility.

Leadership

Exhibits No Evidence		Exhibits Moderate Evidence	Exhibits Significant Evidence

Competency

Exhibits No Evidence		Exhibits Moderate Evidence	Exhibits Significant Evidence

11. Addresses any valid concerns or issues about diversity in a timely manner when available information suggests such an action.

Leadership

Exhibits No Evidence		Exhibits Moderate Evidence	Exhibits Significant Evidence

Competency

Exhibits No Evidence		Exhibits Moderate Evidence	Exhibits Significant Evidence

Organizational Assessment of
Diversity and Leadership

Guidelines: The attached guidelines provide a framework for a holistic and balanced diagnosis of the organization. This assessment should specifically address issues of diversity and student, staff, and faculty success. These guidelines will help an organization focus on the dimensions and actions that contribute to achieving results and will include planning, execution of plans, assessment of progress, and cycles of improvement. These criteria are also nonprescriptive and allow each organization to address their individual character and unique issues and needs without being limited to set practices or specific approaches to achieve the desired results. The questions are intentionally broad and ask for a focused response in three dimensions: (1) the approach-one that is systematic, integrated, and consistency applied; (2) the deployment-the extent to which the approach is applied; and (3) results-the measures of performance and success relative to appropriate comparisons.

Scoring: Each area should be assessed using the attached scoring guidelines. These guidelines will determine the levels of maturity of the approach, deployment, and results within the organization.

Organizational Overview: Before completing this assessment, it would be beneficial for the leadership team to prepare an outline that will identify the characteristics and issues that are unique, relevant, and important to the organization. This will allow each organization flexibility in selecting an approach

consistent with given circumstances. It will also allow the organization to define a set of valid measures of success for each population.

Basic Description: Provide a mission description, the profile of the organization's populations, and the nature of the organization's programs and activities.

Stakeholder/Constituent Requirements: Identify the important stakeholders and their requirements to include specific programs, activities, and services.

Partnerships: Identify special partnership arrangements and their special requirements (if any).

Performance: Identify the principal factors that determine performance success and the performance leaders in similar organizations.

Other Factors: Provide information that describes the unique nature of the organization, new developments, or factors that affect.

Leadership: Describe how leaders provide effective leadership in fostering diversity and success within the organization, taking into account the needs and expectations of all key stakeholders.

- How does the leadership team communicate and clearly incorporate the values of diversity and student, faculty, and staff success in the organization's directions and expectations?

- How does the leadership team communicate the expectations for accountability throughout the organization?

- How does the leadership team seek future opportunities to incorporate and embed the values of diversity and success in the organization?

- How does the leadership team maintain a climate conducive to learning, equity, and success?

- How does the leadership team incorporate the views and efforts of all constituencies (underrepresented and majority) into the leadership system?

Organizational Strategy: Describe how the organization sets strategic direction and how this strategy is translated into action plans and performance requirements

- How are implementation responsibilities decided and assigned?

- How does the organization track organizational performance relative to the plans?

- How are process barriers (that impede progress) identified and incorporated into the strategic plans and actions?

Stakeholder Knowledge/Focus: Describe how the organization determines the requirements and expectations of students, staff, faculty, and other important constituents relative to satisfaction, support, and success

- How does the organization listen and learn from its faculty, staff, students, and other important constituents?

- How are key programs, activities, and services determined or projected into the future?

- How are the relative importance/value of programs, activities, and services determined or projected into the future?

- How are constituent inputs, including retention and complaints, used to improve organizational performance?

Selection and Use of Data and Information: Describe the organization's selection, management, and use of data and information needed to support key processes and to improve organization performance

- What are the main types of data: and information (e.g., instructional, operations and constituent data), and how does each relate and align to the diversity and success goals?

- How are the data and information integrated into the measurements that can be used to track and improve the organization's performance and success?

Education. Training and Development: Describe how the organization's education and training address key organization plans and needs, including building knowledge and capabilities and contributing to improved performance, diversity, development, and success.

- How do education and training address the key performance plans and needs, including longer term employee development?

- How are the education and training designed and delivered?

- How are knowledge and skills reinforced on the job?

Education and Support Processes: Describe how the organization's key processes (educational and support) are designed, managed, and improved to incorporate the themes of diversity and success

- How are key requirements determined or set? (Incorporate inputs from appropriate constituents.)

- How are key educational and support processes designed to meet the overall current and future performance requirements?

- How are the processes managed to maintain process performance and to ensure results will meet the requirements and desired outcomes?

Results: Summarize the results of diversity and measures of success using key measures or indicators of educational and support performance

- Summarize current levels and trends in key measures or indicators of perfor-

mance. Include comparative data (internal or national benchmarks). These measures should include regulatory/legal compliance, as well as others that support the organization's strategy (e.g., new programs or services).

Self-Assessment Scoring Guidelines

Stage 1: Beginning

- There is no systematic approach to respond to the criteria
- Information is anecdotal in nature
- Early stages of gathering data, little to no trend data
- The approach is confined to senior management

Stage 2: Development

- There is the beginning of a systematic approach to address the issues
- The organization is in the early stages of transition from reacting to problems to the early stages of anticipating issues
- Major gaps exist that inhibit progress in achieving the intent of the criteria
- The beginning of a fact-based approach is evident
- Beginning stages of improvement cycles
- The approach extends beyond the senior management
- Little to no compartive data

Stage 3: Sound

- A sound and systematic approach is evi-

dent and responsive to the primary purpose of the criteria

- A fact-based improvement process is in place in key areas
- More emphasis is placed on improving rather than reacting to problems
- Improvement trends or good performance reported in many to most areas
- Organization has comparative data in most key areas

Stage 4: Mature

- A sound and systematic approach responsive to the overall purposes of the criteria
- A fact-based improvements process is a key management tool and clear evidence of cycles of refinement and improvement analysis
- The approach is well-deployed throughout the organization
- Current performance is excellent in most areas with excellent trends
- Organization uses comparative data in all areas and leads or competes favorably in the key areas

Student Survey on Classroom Environment

DIRECTIONS: Please fill in completely with pen (like this: ●) the circle corresponding to your answer to each question.

SEX:	DISABILITY:	GPA:
○ Female	○ Yes	
○ Male	○ No	

AGE:

NUMBER OF SEMESTERS
AT THIS COLLEGE:

PROGRAM (please select one):
- ○ Liberal Arts
- ○ Humanities/Social Science
- ○ Engineering/Computer Science
- ○ Sciences/Mathematics
- ○ Education
- ○ Business/Accounting
- ○ Health Professions
- ○ Other _____

RACE/ETHNICITY:
- ○ African American/Black
- ○ Asian/Pacific Islander
- ○ European American/White
- ○ Hispanic/Latino/Chicano
- ○ Multiracial
- ○ American Indian

	strongly agree	agree	neutral	disagree	strongly disagree	n/a
1. I can contribute to class discussions.	○	○	○	○	○	○
2. When I take notes in class I write down most of the information that is covered by the instructor	○	○	○	○	○	○
3. My instructors show respect for the different ways that students learn.	○	○	○	○	○	○
4. I prefer instruction that includes activities that allow students to interact.	○	○	○	○	○	○
5. Including information about diversity in the curriculum detracts from learning the basic information that must be learned in the course.	○	○	○	○	○	○
6. I prefer instruction that applies course concepts to the real world.	○	○	○	○	○	○
7. The class appreciates the knowledge that I exhibit.	○	○	○	○	○	○
8. I feel comfortable learning information or course content that does not seem familiar to me.	○	○	○	○	○	○
9. Group work in the classroom encourages greater student responsibility for learning course content.	○	○	○	○	○	○
10. My instructors generally treat all students equally.	○	○	○	○	○	○
11. I prefer instruction where student feedback is periodically requested to assess the instructor's effectiveness.	○	○	○	○	○	○
12. In most of my courses the curriculum included real-world and/or practical examples of course content.	○	○	○	○	○	○
13. I am involved in this class.	○	○	○	○	○	○
14. My academic performance is not influenced by the opinions of other students.	○	○	○	○	○	○
15. I prefer to learn new information by working with my instructors and peers in cooperative group activities.	○	○	○	○	○	○
16. Female students are called on more for answers than male students.	○	○	○	○	○	○
17. I prefer instruction which seeks ways to meet students' individual learning needs.	○	○	○	○	○	○

60739

Please do not write here.

over

	strongly agree	agree	neutral	disagree	strongly disagree	n/a
18. The course content that I have been exposed to has helped me to view and understand the perspective of different ethnic and cultural groups.	O	O	O	O	O	O
19. I feel like I belong in this class.	O	O	O	O	O	O
20. I feel comfortable learning information or course content that has relevance for me.	O	O	O	O	O	O
21. Interacting with students in groups exposes me to the learning and thinking strategies of others.	O	O	O	O	O	O
22. My instructors generally exhibit positive interactions with minority/underrepresented students in class.	O	O	O	O	O	O
23. I prefer instruction which includes a variety of teaching approaches.	O	O	O	O	O	O
24. In most of my courses, the curriculum included information about the experiences of various cultural and ethnic groups.	O	O	O	O	O	O
25. I am willing to persist at unstimulating tasks in the classroom.	O	O	O	O	O	O
26. In the classroom when students form groups they prefer to select students who are the same in terms of gender.	O	O	O	O	O	O
27. White male students have more favorable interactions with instructors than minority male students.	O	O	O	O	O	O
28. I prefer instruction that equalizes all students' chances of being successful in the classroom.	O	O	O	O	O	O
29. I prefer instruction which creates an awareness about my own cultural and ethnic identity.	O	O	O	O	O	O
30. The curriculum that I have been exposed to will help me to perform effectively in the workplace.	O	O	O	O	O	O
31. My academic performance is greatly affected when the instructor comments on my abilities.	O	O	O	O	O	O
32. When I take notes in class I focus on specific facts as opposed to writing everything down.	O	O	O	O	O	O
33. In the classroom I tend to lose interest when tasks are boring or unstimulating.	O	O	O	O	O	O
34. In the classroom when students form groups they prefer to select students who are the same in terms of race.	O	O	O	O	O	O
35. The curriculum that I have been exposed to will prepare me to succeed in the global workforce.	O	O	O	O	O	O
36. I prefer instruction which creates an awareness about other students' cultural and ethnic identities.	O	O	O	O	O	O

Please add any additional comments of your own:

60739

INDEX